Gate Theatre presents

IMAGE OF AN UNKNOWN YOUNG WOMAN

by Elinor Cook

T0347753

Image of an Unknown Young Woman was first performed
at the Gate Theatre, London, on 4 June 2015

IMAGE OF AN UNKNOWN YOUNG WOMAN

by Elinor Cook

Cast

in order of appearance

Chorus	Oliver Birch
Chorus	Emilie Patry
Chorus	Isaac Ssebandeke
Yasmin	Eileen Walsh
Leyla	Anjana Vasan
Ali	Ashley Zhangazha
Nia	Wendy Kweh
Candace	Susan Brown

Creative Team

Director	Christopher Haydon
Designer	Fly Davis
Lighting Designer	Mark Howland
Sound Designer	George Dennis
Assistant Director	Lynette Linton
Design Assistant	Magdalena Iwanskaa
Production Manager	Michael Ager
Deputy Stage Manager	Katy Munroe-Farlie
Assistant Stage Manager	Emma Nairne
Press	Kate Morley for
	Kate Morley PR
	kate@katemorleypr.com |
	07970 465648

With special thanks to Katherine Thorogood

This play was developed with the support of the National Theatre Studio.

The Gate would also like to thank the following people for their help with the development of this production: Iona Firouzabadi, Ruth Hawkins, the Gate Theatre's volunteer ushers, the team at Omnibus Clapham, and all those who gave their help after this playtext had gone to print.

Cast

OLIVER BIRCH | CHORUS
Oliver Birch trained at LAMDA. Theatre credits include *Treasure Island, There Is a War* (National Theatre); *Moby Dick, The Cabinet of Dr Caligari, The Four Stages of Cruelty* (Arcola); *Jack and the Beanstalk* (West Yorkshire Playhouse); *66 Books* (Bush); *The Snow Queen* (Dukes Lancaster); *Alice in Wonderland* (Sheffield Crucible); *We All Fall Down* (En Masse Theatre); *A Month in the Country* (Salisbury Playhouse); *Macbeth* (Broadway's Lyceum/West End/Chichester); *Twelfth Night* (Chichester); *Scenes from an Execution* (Sweet Pea Productions);*The Duchess of Malfi* (West Yorkshire Playhouse). Television credits include *In the Flesh* (BBC). Film credits include *Macbeth, Peacock Season*.

SUSAN BROWN | CANDACE
Theatre credits include *Good People* (Noël Coward); *Julius Caesar* (Donmar at St Ann's Warehouse, New York); *Making Noise Quietly, The Wild Duck* (Donmar Warehouse); *Saved* (Lyric Hammersmith); *If You Don't Let Us Dream We Won't Let You Sleep, Goodbye To All That, Seagulls, Gibraltar Strait, Downfall, Shirley, Road* (Royal Court); *Harper Regan, The Hour We Knew Nothing of Each Other, Playing with Fire, Henry IV Parts I & II, Cardiff East* (National Theatre); *Bad Weather, Easter, Romeo and Juliet, Richard III* (RSC); *Dying For It, Butterfly Kiss* (Almeida); *The Contingency Plan* (Bush); *The Chairs, The House of Bernarda Alba* (Gate); *You Be Ted and I'll Be Sylvia* (Hampstead); *Small Change, Iphigenia* (Sheffield Crucible); *The Beaux' Stratagem, Back Me to Methuselah, The Vortex, The Way of the World, A Woman of No Importance* (Cambridge Theatre Company); *Playing Sinatra* (Warehouse/Greenwich); *Twelfth Night* (ETT). Film credits include *Belle, The Iron Lady, Now is Good, Brideshead Revisited, Hope and Glory*.

WENDY KWEH | NIA
Trained: Royal Academy of Dramatic Art. Theatre credits include *Chimerica, Othello, Romeo and Juliet, Boeing Boeing, Much Ado About Nothing, The Office Party, A Midsummer Night's Dream, Moonwalking in Chinatown, The Oresteia, The Little Shop of Horrors, Broken Birds*. Film credits include *Snowden, Hot Hot Hot, The Blue Mansion*. Television credits include *Apocalypse Slough, Holby City, Coronation Street, Casualty, Murder City, The Year of the Tiger,The Crooked Man, The Bill, Doctors*. Radio credits include *Demolition Man, Words and Music, Bare Branches, Boom, Westway*.

EMILIE PATRY | CHORUS
Emilie trained at the Central School of Speech and Drama and at the Studio 34 in Paris. Theatre credits include *The Gamblers* (Greyscale, UK tour); *A Beginning, Middle and an End* (Traverse/Tron/Hull Truck); *Stars in the Morning Sky* (Riverside Studios); *Can't Stand Up For Falling Down* (Arcola); *Macbeth* (New Wimbledon); *Les Isles Kerguelen* (Théatre De La Tempête, Paris); *Bastringue* (L'Etoile du Nord, Paris). Television credits include *Casualty 1907* (BBC); *Behind Closed Doors* (BBC Scotland); *The Advocates* (STV) and *Gayle Tuesday: The Comeback* (Living TV). She is co-founder of Jagged Fence Theatre Company.

ISAAC SSEBANDEKE | CHORUS

Theatre credits include *The Taming of the Shrew* (Two Gents); *We Are Proud to Present…* (Bush; Off West End Winner: Best Ensemble); *One Monkey Don't Stop No Show* (Eclipse). Television credits include *Cucumber, Dubplate Drama* (Channel 4); *Casualty, The Well, Doctors* (BBC); *The Dumping Ground* (CBBC). Film credits include *Shoot Me* (Palladio Films); *Columbite Tantalite* (dir. Chiwetel Ejiofor). Isaac is also a writer and his debut play *My Darling Wife* was shortlisted for the inaugural Adrian Pagan Award 2013 before receiving a staged reading at Talawa's New Writing Festival, Talawa Firsts 2014.

ANJANA VASAN | LEYLA

Anjana Vasan trained at the Royal Welsh College of Music and Drama. Theatre credits include: For the National Theatre: *Dara, Behind the Beautiful Forevers*. For the RSC: *The Taming of the Shrew, Much Ado About Nothing*. Other theatre credits include *Macbeth, Golgotha, The Radicalistion of Bradley Manning, Rhinoceros, 66 Books, Me and Bessie*. Television credits include *Fresh Meat, Asia at War Fighting for India*. Film credits include *Cinderella, Black + White + Silence* (short).

EILEEN WALSH | YASMIN

Recent theatre credits include *Lippy, Teh Internet is Serious Business, The Believers, Liolà, Sand, Hamlet* and many moons ago, *Disco Pigs*. Film credits include *Magdalene Sisters* and more recently *Catastrophe* for Channel 4.

ASHLEY ZHANGAZHA | ALI

Trained at the Guildhall School of Music and Drama. Theatre credits include *Ah, Wilderness!* (Young Vic); *Hamlet* (Manchester Royal Exchange); *Venice Preserv'd* (The Spectators Guild); *Henry V* (Michael Grandage Company); *Fences* (Duchess/Theatre Royal Bath); *Macbeth* (Sheffield Crucible); *Belong, truth and reconciliation* (Royal Court); *Richard II, King Lear* (Donmar Warehouse); *Danton's Death* (National Theatre); *Oliver* (London Palladium); *Whistle Down the Wind* (Aldwych); and he is an alumni of the National Youth Theatre. Television credits include *Humans* (Channel 4) and *Ordinary Lies* (BBC1). Radio credits include *Rasselas, Prince of Abyssinia* (BBC Radio 4). Awarded 1st prize Ian Charleson Award after *Macbeth* (Sheffield Crucible) and Ian Charleson Commendation after *King Lear* (Donmar Warehouse).

Creative

ELINOR COOK | WRITER

Elinor was the winner of the George Devine Award 2013 for Most Promising Playwright. *The Boy Preference* will feature as part of the 2015 National Theatre Connections programme this summer. Elinor is currently writing an adaptation of Eleanor Catton's novel, *The Rehearsal*, for LAMDA. Will Wrightson is attached to direct. She was also recently selected by the Gate Theatre to take part in Warwick Arts Centre's 2015 this_is_tomorrow residency, in connection with China Plate Theatre and the University of Warwick. *The Girl's Guide to Saving the World* was produced by HighTide as part of their festival in April 2014, directed by Amelia Sears. Elinor wrote an episode of *The Secrets* for Working Title Television, which was directed by Dominic Savage on BBC One. In 2012 Elinor was part of the Royal Court's 'Supergroup' and Paines Plough's 'The Big Room' in association with Channel 4. *This is Where We Got When You Came In*, an interactive performance, co-written by Elinor and Non Zero One was the Bush Theatre's final production in their old home. It was awarded Best Entertainment at the Off West End Awards. Prior to her writing career, Elinor was the senior reader at the Royal Court Theatre from 2007–2009.

MICHAEL AGER | PRODUCTION MANAGER

Michael is a freelance Theatre Production Manager. He previously worked at the Young Vic Theatre as Technician and Production Manager for the Taking Part Department (2007–2013), where he production managed numerous projects with young people, schools, local community and young directors in the Clare and Maria Theatres. Previous credits for The Gate: *Eclipsed*, *The Edge of Our Bodies*, *The Rise and Shine of Comrade Fiasco*. Recent productions include *Man* (Young Vic); *Flat Stanley* (Engine House); *Who Do We Think We Are?* (Visible Ensemble); *The Saints and the Best Christmas Present in the World* (Nuffield Playing Field, Southampton); *In Lambeth* (Spell Bound Productions); *Debris* (Open Works); *The Cutting of the Cloth*, *London Wall*, *What the Women Did* (Two's Company Productions); *Tutto Bene Mama*, *The Last Yankee*, *Ignis* (The Print Room); *Donny's Brain*, *Godchild*, *Fault Lines*, *The Blackest Black and In the Vale of Health* (Hampstead); *Early Days* (*Of a Better Nation*) (for Coney at Battersea Arts Centre, Warwick Arts Centre and Frascati Theater Amstersam).

FLY DAVIS | SET AND COSTUME DESIGNER

Training: RADA, Motley. Design credits include *I'd Rather Goya Robbed Me of My Sleep Than Some Other Arsehole* (Gate); *Scuttlers*, *Hunger for Trade* (Manchester Royal Exchange); *James and the Giant Peach* (West Yorkshire Playhouse); *Turning a Little Further*, *A Streetcar Named Desire* (Young Vic, Clare); *Eye of a Needle*, *Superior Donuts* (Southwark Playhouse); *The Dissidents* (Tricycle); *Primetime*, *Pigeons*, *Collaboration* (Royal Court); *The Great British Countryfile Fete* (Bush); *Dracula*: *Mr Swallow The Musical* (Soho); *Awkward Conversations with Animals I F*cked* (Underbelly); *Khadika is 18*, *Almost Near*, *The Man* (Finborough); *The Wonderful World of Dissocia*, *White Guard* (Drama Centre); *England Street* (Oxford Playhouse); *Woyzeck* (Omnibus); *What the Animals Say* (Greyscale). *Love is Easy* (McFly music video). Fly is currently designing *The Crocodile* (Manchester International Festival); *The Comedy of Errors* (schools tour National Theatre); *I Want My Hat Back* (National Theatre); and *The Glass Menagerie* (Headlong). As

Associate Designer: *Mr Burns* (Almeida); *Disconnect, No Quarter, Open Court Season, The Twits* (Royal Court) .

This role is funded by the Jerwood Charitable Foundation, as part of the Jerwood Young Designers Programme at the Gate.

GEORGE DENNIS | SOUND DESIGNER

Previous Gate Theatre credits include: *Eclipsed, The Edge of Our Bodies, Dances of Death.* Theatre credits include *Eclipsed* (Gate); *Beautiful Thing* (West End/UK tour); *Fireworks, Liberian Girl* (Royal Court); *A Breakfast of Eels, The Last Yankee* (Print Room); *peddling* (Arcola /59E59, New York/HighTide Festival); *Visitors* (Bush); *Regeneration* (Royal & Derngate/UK tour); *Mametz* (National Theatre of Wales); *Minotaur* (Polka/Clwyd Theatr Cymru); *Spring Awakening* (Headlong); *The Island* (Young Vic); *Love Your Soldiers* (Sheffield Crucible Studio); *Thark* (Park); *Moth* (Bush/HighTide Festival); *Hello/Goodbye* (Hampstead Downstairs); *Liar Liar* (Unicorn); *Good Grief* (Theatre Royal Bath/UK tour); *The Seven Year Itch* (Salisbury Playhouse); *When Did You Last See My Mother?* (Trafalgar Studios 2); *The Living Room* (Jermyn Street); *Debris, The Seagull, The Only True History of Lizzie Finn* (Southwark Playhouse); *A Life, Foxfinder* (Finborough).

CHRISTOPHER HAYDON | DIRECTOR

Christopher is Artistic Director at the Gate Theatre. Credits include: *The Edge of Our Bodies, Grounded, Trojan Women, Purple Heart, The Prophet, Wittenburg* (Gate); *Twelve Angry Men* (Birmingham Rep/West End); *Sixty-Six Books, In the Beginning* (Bush/Westminster Abbey); *A Safe Harbour for Elizabeth Bishop* (Southbank Centre); *Grace, Pressure Drop* (On Theatre); *Deep Cut* (Sherman Cymru/national tour); *Monsters, Notes from Underground* (Arcola); *A Number* (Salisbury Playhouse).

MARK HOWLAND | LIGHTING DESIGNER

Mark studied, briefly, at Oxford University prior to training in Stage Lighting Design at RADA. Previous credits for the Gate include *Eclipsed, Purple Heart, The Trojan Women, The Prophet, The Kreutzer Sonata* (2012 revival), *Yerma, Wittenberg, The Kreutzer Sonata* (2009), *Vanya.* Other theatre credits include *Hitchcock Blonde* (Hull Truck); *Ignorance* (Hampstead); *Canvas* (Chichester Festival); *Ghosts, Sweeney Todd* (Aarhus Theatre, Denmark); *Singing in the Rain* (New Theatre, Copenhagen); *Entertaining Mr. Sloane, One Flew Over the Cuckoo's Nest, Absurd Person Singular, Molly Sweeney, Translations* (Curve); *Measure for Measure* (Sherman Cymru); *Bea, Pressure Drop, On Religion* (On Theatre); *Six Dance Lessons in Six Weeks* (Vienna's English Theatre); *Dick Turpin's Last Ride, Much Ado About Nothing, Cider with Rosie, The Merchant of Venice* (Theatre Royal Bury St Edmunds); *The Man Jesus, Uncle Vanya, Dockers, The Home Place* (Lyric, Belfast); *A Number* (Salisbury Playhouse); *Topless Mum* (Tobacco Factory); *Monsters* (Arcola); *The Pains of Youth* (Belgrade Theatre).

MAGDALENA IWANSKAA | DESIGN ASSISTANT

Magdalena Iwanska received her degree for Design for Stage from the Royal Central School of Speech and Drama. She is a freelance costume and set designer for stage and screen. Working across a variety of disciplines Magdalena is passionate about design that's captivating, playful and interactive; transforming the space and telling a story of its own. Her credits include set design for *Love and Information* at Embassy Theatre directed by Richard Beecham, *Before the Night is Through* at Landor Theatre directed by Rob McWhirl and *Widows* at Webber Douglas Studio directed by Dominic Rouse.

This role is funded by the Jerwood Charitable Foundation, as part of the Jerwood Young Designers Programme at the Gate.

LYNETTE LINTON | ASSISTANT DIRECTOR

Lynette Linton is a director, and playwright. She trained on the StoneCrabs Young Directors Course where she was also awarded the Jack Petchy Award. Directing credits include *Naked* by Jessica Burgess (Vault Festival 2015), *Pornado* (Theatre Royal Stratford East), *This Wide Night* (Albany), *Stunted*, (Rehearsed Reading, Theatre Royal Stratford East) and Co-Director on *Chicken Shop* (Royal & Derngate, Theatre Royal Stratford East). As Assistant Director: *Gutted* (Theatre Royal Stratford East). Her writing has been performed at venues such as Theatre Royal Stratford East, Soho and Bush Theatre. Her new play *Chicken Palace*, will be at a site-specific location in association with Theatre Royal Stratford East in August 2015.

KATY MUNROE-FARLIE | DEPUTY STAGE MANAGER

Katy Munroe-Farlie graduated from the University of Hull in 2010 with a Degree in Theatre and Performance. From there she became the resident Stage and Production Manager for the New End Theatre until August 2011 before becoming freelance. Other shows for the Gate include *Eclipsed, The Chronicles of Kalki, Grounded* (also national and international tour), *Body of an American* (also Royal & Derngate, Northampton), *Purple Heart, The Trojan Women.* Other credits include *Deathship 666* (Leicester Square Theatre); *Zelda, Barbershopera* (Trafagar Studios 2); *These Trees are Made of Blood, The Illusion, The Hairy Ape, Shivered* (Southwark Playhouse); *Twelfth Night* (Minack); *Herding Cats* (Hampstead Downstairs); *Blue Surge* (Finborough); *Bunny* (Soho Theatre Upstairs); *Mr Happiness and the Water Engine* (Old Vic Tunnels).

EMMA NAIRNE | ASSISTANT STAGE MANAGER

Emma graduated from the University of Plymouth with a BSc in Psychology in 2009. Her career in theatre began at the Edinburgh Fringe Festival, where she will return this summer for the sixth year, working for The Pleasance. Most recently Emma has been working as a Stage Manager on the UK tour of *Grumpy Old Women* (Emma Brünjes Productions); *Jekyll & Hyde* (Sell A Door, UK tour) and *The Boy Who Kicked Pigs* (Kill The Beast, UK tour). Other professional Stage Management highlights include *The Snail and the Whale* (Tall Stories, UK and North America tour); *The Heads* (Blind Summit/Soho); *The Table* (Blind Summit/France tour); *Sex with a Stranger* (Invisible Dot Ltd, Trafalgar Studios); *Peppa Pig's Party Live!* (Limelight Ltd, UK and Ireland tour); *Return to the Silence* (Curious Directive, Pleasance Theatre). Emma has also worked extensively with the Guildford School of Acting on productions including *Lucky Stiff, Gut Girls, Merrily We Roll Along* and *The Hot Mikado.*

The Gate is committed to being environmentally responsible. In line with our GreenGate policy the C02 from the manufacture and distribution of paper used for the printing of these playtexts is captured by planting trees with the Woodland Trust. If you're finished with it, why not donate this book to a charity shop, or recycle where possible. To find out more about our GreenGate policy please visit **www.gatetheatre.co.uk**

Jerwood Young Designers

Since 2001 Jerwood Young Designers has given outstanding individuals the opportunity to lead on the design of the productions at the Gate Theatre in Notting Hill. In 2013, acknowledging the creative ambition of the Gate's productions, this programme grew to include support for design assistants. For *Image of an Unknown Young Woman*, this has meant supporting Fly Davis as Designer, with additional support from Magdalena Iwanskaa, Design Assistant.

The Gate has long had a reputation as one of the most versatile studio spaces in London, perfect for designers to explore theatrical possibilities. They also have the chance to work with some of the finest directors and writers working in theatre, an experience which is invaluable in establishing reputation and contacts.

The support that the Jerwood Young Designers Programme provides in both nurturing talent and offering the opportunity of practical experience has been instrumental in launching the careers of some of the country's most exciting theatrical designers.

By the end of the 2015/16 programme, Jerwood will have supported 76 placements on the Young Designers Programme over the course of 14 years.

www.jerwoodcharitablefoundation.org

JERWOOD
CHARITABLE FOUNDATION

About the Gate Theatre

'London's most relentlessly ambitious theatre' *Time Out*

The Gate sits above the Prince Albert pub in Notting Hill, and has been inspiring audiences and artists alike for 35 years. We are a small theatre but we always Think Big.

We are a home for anarchic spirits, invigorating theatre, and restless creative ambition. We welcome anyone who wants to change the world. In our ever transformable, 75-seat space we confront and debate the biggest questions that face humanity and act as a loudspeaker for unheard voices from across the globe. We are known to springboard the most exceptional new talent into becoming the theatre leaders of tomorrow.

No two visits to the Gate are ever the same.

Artistic Director	**Christopher Haydon**
Executive Director	**Clare Slater**
Associate Director*	**Tinuke Craig**
Producer	**Daisy Cooper**
Associate Producer*	**Nina Segal**
General Manager	**Steve Sargeant/Chrissy Angus**
Development Manager	**Fiona English**
Technical Manager*	**Andrew Rungen**
Finance Manager*	**Lindsay Nock**
Administrator	**Suzy Sancho**
Intern*	**Natasha Brown**
Venue Technician	**Rich Hoxley**

*Indicates part-time role

Front of House
Pippa Davis, Esther Huntington, Eloise Green, Zoe Lambrachis, Chloe France, Rike Berge, Katy Munroe-Farlie, Nick Hafezi, Bradley Connor, Katy Hills, Kieran Lucas, Annabel Williamson, Chiara Ciabattoni, Eleanor Rose, Susan Keats, Hannah Forrester, Cecily Rabey

Associate Artists
Lucy Ellinson, Rachel Chavkin, Ellen McDougall, Clare Slater, Oliver Townsend, Charlotte Westenra

The Gate Theatre Company is a company limited by guarantee.
Registered in England & Wales No. 1495543 | Charity No. 280278
Registered address: 11 Pembridge Road, Above the Prince Albert Pub,
London, W11 3HQ

Supported using public funding by
**ARTS COUNCIL
ENGLAND**

You hold the key to the Gate

The Gate Theatre sits above the Prince Albert Pub at the heart of Notting Hill, and has been inspiring audiences and artists alike for 35 years. We are a small theatre but we always Think Big.

We are a home for free spirits, invigorating theatre, and restless creative ambition. We welcome anyone who wants to change the world. In our ever transformable, 75-seat space we confront and debate the biggest questions that face humanity and act as a loudspeaker for unheard voices from across the globe.

We are a 'teaching theatre' for emerging talent and are constantly seeking to grow and deepen our impact on artists, audiences, our local community and the wider British theatre industry.

Each year, to maintain our programming and achieve our aspirations, the Gate needs to raise a third of its income through private fundraising, form supporters like you. This year, that figure is £225,000. Your support means we can keep telling these challenging stories, in an intimate space, on an epic scale.

Did you know?

- We are a registered charity (number 280278) and we need to raise £225,000 a year.

- We employ over 125 emerging artists and technicians a year.

- 17,684 saw a Gate production in 2014/15: 10,809 people came to the Gate and a further 9,338 saw *Grounded* either in Washington DC, Sweden or across the UK.

- Rachel Weisz, Jude Law and Colin Farrell all acted at the Gate at the start of their careers. Rufus Norris, Stephen Daldry, Rupert Goold, Katie Mitchell, Dominic Cooke, and Erica Whyman all directed here. Tom Scutt, Soutra Gilmpir, Naomi Dawson, Jon Bausor and Max Jones designed at the Gate. Careers start at the Gate.

- Over 1,000 young artists take part in our Gate Educate programme each year.

- Without private and public support, a ticket to the Gate would cost £53. Thanks to our donors, our average ticket price in 2014/15 was just £15.36 helping us remain affordable to a diverse audience from all walks of life.

For more information on how you can support the Gate's work, please visit www.gatetheatre.co.uk or contact us on 020 7229 5387 or email Fiona English, Development Manager, at fiona@gatetheatre.co.uk

The Gate would like to thank the following for their continued generous support

GATE GUARDIANS
Katrina and Chris Barter, Geraldine and Chris Brodie, Tim and Amy Bevan, Lauren and Michael Clancy, Richard and Jan Grandison, James Hughes-Hallett, Helen and Paul Jameson, Addy Loudiadis, Kate Maltby, Miles Morland, Nicola and James Reed, Jon and NoraLee Sedmak, The Emmanuel Kaye Foundation

GATE AMBASSADORS
Caroline and Jim Clark, Nick and Jane Ferguson, Penny and Barry Francis, Thomas and Julie Hoegh, David and Abigail Lacey, David and Linda Lakhdhir, Georgia Oetker, Ellen and Michel Plantevin, Charles and Barbara Prideaux, Scott Stevens and Eva Boenders, Jan Topham, The Ulrich Family

GATE KEEPERS
Tina and Habib Achkar, The Agency (London) Ltd., Matthew Bannister, Paula Marie Black, Christiane and Bruno Boesch, Ariane Braillard, Neil and Sarah Brener, Sarah and Phillippe Chappatte, Charles Cormick, Robert Devereux, David Emmerson, Joachim Fleury, Tony Mackintosh, Andy McIntyre, Elisabeth Morse, Lyndsey Posner, Mark and Claire Ralf, Joyce Reuben, Pascale Revert and Peter Wheeler, Mark Robinson, David and Susie Sainsbury, Paul and Caroline Weiland

GATE YOUNG SUPPORTERS NETWORK
Ella Kaye, Kate Maltby

Thank you to all our Gate Openers, Gate New Plays Fund, Directors' Appeal and Production Syndicate supporters too.

TRUSTS AND FOUNDATIONS
Arts Council England, Backstage Trust, Fidelio, Jerwood Charitable Foundation, Royal Borough of Kensington & Chelsea, The Emmanuel Kaye Foundation, The Fenton Arts Trust, The Goldsmiths' Company, The Mercers' Company and the Wates Foundation.

CORPORATE SUPPORTERS
The Shed Restaurant, Rien Qui Bonge, Polpo Notting Hill

Special thanks to Jenny Hall

IMAGE OF AN UNKNOWN YOUNG WOMAN

Elinor Cook

Characters

CHORUS
A, *female/male, any age*
B, *female/male, any age*
C, *female/male, any age*

One member of the chorus should be female and in her twenties

YASMIN, *female, any age from late teens to thirties*
LEYLA, *female, twenties*
ALI, *male, twenties*
CANDACE, *female, late fifties*
NIA, *female, forties*
GIRL IN THE YELLOW DRESS, *female, twenties – A, B or C can play the role here; whoever fits age-wise.*

This text went to press before the end of rehearsals and so may differ slightly from the play as performed.

 # 1

The sound of a girl breathing through a tube.

The beep of a heart monitor.

It gets louder and louder and then –

 # 2

A, B *and* C *enter.*

They look at each other and then begin.

A	Everyone stop what you're doing. And watch this. Now.
B	This is happening. This *just* happened.
C	What did?
B	This literally just happened right now.
C	Sorry. What did??
A	Warning. The following contains content some viewers may find upsetting.
C	Goddam you shitty WIFI!
B	Are you watching? Skype me and tell me if you're watching.
C	It's blocked on my – Cos I didn't update the –

	I need to know this SECOND what it is that just happened.
B	PLEASE EVERYONE STOP AND WATCH AND SHARE.
A	Have *you* watched it?
C	Uh, of *course* I have.
B	I just saw it. God…
A	Terrible.
C	Reprehensible.
A	It just flashed up. It literally just flashed up on my screen.
C	That poor girl.
B	What girl?
A	It just flashed up!
C	You have to watch it right through to the end, OK.
B	But it keeps freezing. Why, WHY does it keep – ?
A	Have you seen the bit where she sort of crumples to her knees?
B	Yes I've seen *that* bit.
C	And when she puts her hands over her stomach and, Christ –
A	All that red, red blood –
C	Yes, it sort of arcs out of her.
A	A lot of very red, very thick, very *pleasing* actually –
B	That lovely girl in yellow.
C	What?

B	The girl in the yellow dress.
A	I'm not sure what you –
C	You haven't seen it?!
A	Not yet.
C	Google it. Google it right now.
A	But I'm eating –
C	Right NOW.
B	What so she just – ?
A	Wait. So – Someone shot her?
B	This is disgraceful.
A	Someone just like SHOT her?!
B	I'm disgusted. I'm actually nauseous.
C	In the protests.
B	What protests?
C	God, do you not *listen* to the *Today Programme*??
B	Oh yeah of course. The protests. In – ?
C	She was protesting. She was a protester.
B	Yup. Got it.
A	That's – Yeah, that's a lot of blood.
C	Campaigning for her rights. Democracy.

	Freedom.
	They don't really have them over there.
B	Is she actually dead?
C	So pretty.
A	She *is* pretty isn't she.
C	It's such a shame.
	The prime of her life!
B	Do you know, she actually looks a bit like my friend Emily.
	God I should really call her.
C	And that dress!
	It's so glam.
A	Are those –
	Are those her knickers?
B	What?!
A	Look, if you look –
	You can see her knickers.
C	You shouldn't be looking!
A	I'm sorry but!
	You see a girl's knickers, you look at them.
C	She's bleeding profusely from her stomach!
B	(Can someone possibly –
	Fill me in on the context?)
C	Why would you be paying any attention to her crotch area?!
B	(Hey so.
	Do you know basically what it's all *about*?)
A	What what's about?
B	(Well, I'm a bit behind in, you know –
	Current affairs.)
A	Tsk.
	They're seizing power.

From a government that has countlessly failed to
acknowledge them.

B   Wow OK.

A   A corrupt government.
           An increasingly out of touch yet iron-fisted
           government.

C   Oppression.

A   Yes obviously oppression.

B   What on earth are you doing?

C   Nothing.

B   You're searching for yellow dresses on ASOS?!

C   No I'm –

B   You are!

C   OK fine.
           But I've got my cousin's wedding, haven't I!

A   These horrible, infamous prisons.
           Full of the people who bravely buck against the
           system.
           Terrible.

B   You're actually an awful person.

C   Oh calm down.

B   A terrible, vapid, shallow human being.

A   Hunger strikes are common.
           Torture.
           They get beaten on the soles of their feet.

B   On the soles of their feet?

C   Yes.
           With paddles.
           Repeatedly, not terribly hard, but enough to send
           you slowly mad.

A   Well I tell you what, I REFUSE to watch it.

B	Wait. What?
C	I said I refuse to watch it.
B	Why in heaven's name – ?
C	Because it's prurient.
B	Oh, honestly.
C	It's, it's GHOULISH.
A	Ohhh I think that's a tad harsh!
B	Dying is intimate. Right? It's private. It's not something you should have to share with millions and millions of –
C	Yes but what if it changes perceptions?
A	Yes! Exactly.
C	Raises awareness? Strengthens resolve!
A	It's practically your duty to watch it. *I* think.
B	Yeah but the thing is you're getting off on it.
A	Pardon?
C	What did you say?!
B	She's blonde –
A	Dyed blonde, I reckon.
C	Eh?
A	You can see the roots. If you look.
B	Anyway. She's blonde –
A	(Ish.)

B	And she's thin and she's writhing around and you can see her knickers.
A	She's not actually dead.
C	She isn't?
A	She didn't die.
C	Oh. Oh right.
A	Look here's a picture of her in hospital.
C	Oh God that's nasty. All those tubes coming out of her –
B	So, wait, she DIDN'T die?
C	Well no. Not yet.
B	Oh.
A	Anyway back to my original point.
C	Which is?
B	Oh God I don't know. I'm just a bit shocked that's all.
A	Well yes it's shocking.
B	Really shocking.
A	Look at all those angry people. God.
B	God they're really angry.
C	It's understandable.
A	All those old women weeping. Terrible.
B	Boys weeping too. And men.
C	They're all weeping.
B	Do we know her name?

C	I really want to know her name.
A	Have you shared it?
B	What?
A	SO important, please share.
B	Oh God yes, share, you've got to share.
C	Watch now, so important.
A	SHARE THIS NOW.
B	Just shared it, mate.
C	Awesome, dude.
B	No problem, buddy.
A	Dying for a cause. Wow. Is there a cause that I'd die for?
B	Of course there is!
C	Dunno. Is there?
B	You'd die for democracy! You'd die for justice!
C	Oh yeah. Yeah course I would.
A	She looks a bit like my friend Natalie.
B	She looks a lot like my friend Clare.
C	Changed my profile pic.
B	What?
A	Change your profile pic, can't you?!
C	Cos, in a way, we're all the girl in the yellow dress. I mean, aren't we?
B	We *are* all the girl in the yellow dress.
A, B, C	WE ARE ALL THE GIRL IN THE YELLOW DRESS!

 # 3

A, B and C *gather strips of yellow cloth.*

They tie the cloth around their wrists and over their mouths.

The sound of a huge crowd.

YASMIN *enters – dressed plainly and a little scruffily.*

She hasn't brushed her hair and isn't wearing any make-up.

She has a pile of papers in her hand – roughly photocopied, curling around the edges.

She clears her throat.

She takes the top piece of paper off the pile, then wedges the rest between her knees.

She holds up the piece of paper.

YASMIN   Has anyone seen this – ?
Um.

She has to fight against the noise of the crowd.

Has anyone seen this woman?
Uh –
Hello?

It's too noisy.

EXCUSE ME.
Can you all please, um...
Just, be on the lookout or –
Can you keep your eyes peeled, please...?

No one.

She approaches A *and taps her/him on the shoulder.*

Hi.
Excuse me.
Sorry to, but...
This is my mum.
If you could take a look – ?

A   What?

YASMIN   Does she look familiar to you at all?

A   Listen, can you get phone signal?

YASMIN   Um.

A   Look at this!
           Nothing!

YASMIN   Uh-huh.
           OK it's just I haven't seen her for a bit and I'm
           just trying to…
           Trying to trace her movements or something so –

A   They're here somewhere but I just –
           I can't get through to them.

YASMIN   Um.

A   Everything's blocked.
           The whole network.

YASMIN   Uh-huh.
           Look –

A   Do you think it's them?
           Do you think they've shut it down?

YASMIN   Can I give you one of these?

A   Of course it's them.
           Why am I even asking?

           A *takes the piece of paper.*

           What's this?

           The phone rings.

           A *drops the piece of paper.*

           (*Into phone.*) Where are you?
           No I said where *are* you?

YASMIN   OK.
           Thanks.
           Thank you.

           YASMIN *turns to* B, *who is tapping feverishly
           into a mobile phone.*

Excuse me, hi, have you seen this woman?

She taps B *on the shoulder.*

B *ignores her.*

YASMIN *starts to tuck the piece of paper in* B*'s pocket.*

B   What are you doing?

YASMIN   Sorry to bother you, I'm *Yasmin*, I'm just –

B   Did you take something?

YASMIN   What?

B   From my pocket?
           Just now?

YASMIN   No.

B   Come on, what did you take?

           Beat.

YASMIN   Right, so, this is my mum.

B   What?

YASMIN   This is a picture of –

B   This is your mum?

YASMIN   Have you seen her?
           Recently?

           B *studies the picture.*

B   Sorry I just –
           You feel a hand in your pocket, you make
           assumptions –

YASMIN   That's OK.
           If you could just look…?

           B *studies the picture.*

B   Sorry, but there are a lot of people here and –
           She looks like a lot of people's mums.

YASMIN   Right.
              Well, she looks like my mum.

B   I mean, I'll keep hold of this.

YASMIN   Thank you – ?

B   But, you know, everyone here is looking for
              someone and –

YASMIN   She has a scar.
              If you look –

B   Oh yeah.
              God.
              Bit nasty.

YASMIN   A dog bit her.

B   Right.

YASMIN   For no reason!
              It just jumped up and bit her.

C   What's going on?
              What's this?

YASMIN   It's a picture of –

B   Her mum.

C   Oh right.
              Oh shit.

YASMIN   Could I give you a pile – ?

C   You can't find her?

YASMIN   No.
              But –

C   How long?

YASMIN   Well.
              Day before yesterday.

C   You tried the hospital?

              Beat.

YASMIN   Not yet.

C	I reckon you should try the hospital.
YASMIN	No I don't think – I think she's probably just stuck somewhere. Cos of the blockades maybe.
C	They're coming down pretty heavy, you know.
YASMIN	She's probably inches away, do you know what I mean?!
C	Whereabouts was she protesting?
YASMIN	Oh she wasn't protesting.
C	What?
YASMIN	She just tried to go to the shops. But the ones nearest us, there was nothing in them. Like, just a few bits of rice on the floor. So she said she'd be going a bit further than normal.

A *gets another phone call.*

A	(*Into phone.*) What? I can't hear you –
B	She wasn't protesting?
YASMIN	No.
C	Why not?
YASMIN	Well because –
A	(*Into phone.*) Listen the signal's TERRIBLE so –
YASMIN	She went across town. Where there's a bit more choice and everything. But –
A	(*Into phone.*) Yeah a bit better. YES I CAN HEAR YOU NOW.
YASMIN	I mean, I said *I'd* go. Cos it's normally me that does it. The shopping.

B *tries to remain focused on* YASMIN *but starts tapping at her/his phone nonetheless.*

But she seemed a bit restless or something.
A bit anxious, I don't know.
So I let her do it.
She said she'd be back in half an hour.
But she –
Wasn't.

B   Signal!
               Look, signal!

C   Let me see?

YASMIN   I should have gone though.
               I should have gone.

B   Maybe she's staying with a relative or –
               Oh GOD it's gone again!

YASMIN   I'm not sure what to –
               What do I do?

B   Sorry?

YASMIN   Who should I be talking to?
               Can you help?

A *brandishes her/his phone.*

A   OK!
               There's going to be a vigil outside the hospital.

B   Now?

A   We've got to get to the front.

B   Is it safe?

A   Of course it isn't safe.
               What do you think?

C   We'll go through the shopping mall.
               It'll be quicker.

A   Less police.

B   Do you think?

A   Come on.

A, B and C begin to exit hastily.

The pieces of paper given to them by YASMIN *float, abandoned, to the floor.*

YASMIN *slowly gathers up the pieces of paper.*

She sits down, holding the piece of paper up.

The sound of the crowd surges.

4

LEYLA *and* ALI.

Their apartment.

ALI   I'm going to delete it.

LEYLA   What?

ALI   I'm taking it down.

LEYLA   No.

ALI   I should never have put it up it's –

LEYLA   It's fucking brave, is what it is.

ALI   It's –
            Do you think?

LEYLA   Yes!

ALI   No it's not, it's invasive.
            It's wrong.

LEYLA   OK.
            So you witness something like that –
            You capture something like that on *film* and then
            you just, what?
            Press *delete*?
            No!

ALI	She has no idea. She has no idea what she's started.
LEYLA	You *make* people watch it.
ALI	She's comatose in a hospital bed and she has no idea.
LEYLA	You grab everyone by the scruff of the neck and say, LOOK AT WHAT IS HAPPENING HERE.

Pause.

ALI	It's just sad, that's all. It's just fucking sad.
LEYLA	Yeah.
ALI	That this is what it takes.
LEYLA	You don't have to tell me how fucked up that is.
ALI	Why does some girl have to bleed from a hole in her stomach to get people to pay attention?
LEYLA	Because the world sucks.
ALI	And, OK, while we're asking questions – Why did I just stand there with my fucking camera?
LEYLA	It was a good instinct.
ALI	Why didn't I – I don't know. Why didn't I put her in the recovery position? Why didn't I take off my shirt and try and stop the blood?
LEYLA	Well. People were all over her.
ALI	*That* would have been a good instinct.
LEYLA	You wouldn't have been able to get close. You wouldn't, Ali –

ALI   But no.
            I just stood there.
            I pressed record and I just stood there.

LEYLA   You did something huge.

ALI   No.

LEYLA   You bore witness.

ALI   But a film is never going to –
            It's never going to capture what it was actually
            like.

            Pause.

LEYLA   No.

ALI   You weren't there.

LEYLA   I know.
            I should have been.

ALI   It was so –
            It was shocking.

LEYLA   People constantly miss dentist appointments.
            But not me, apparently.

ALI   I've never even *heard* gunfire before.
            Let alone…

LEYLA   I was going to come afterwards.
            You know that, right?

ALI   She made a noise.
            When it –
            Hit.

LEYLA   You said.

ALI   Like a kind of –
            Surprised noise.
            Like, she sounded *astonished*.

LEYLA   Yeah.

ALI   And then the way she just –
            Sank onto her knees.

	And then her eyes – God.
LEYLA	Yeah.
ALI	The way they – Suddenly she wasn't a person any more, almost. She was like something in a horror film. *She* was horrifying. God, is that why I couldn't touch her?
LEYLA	You, I don't know, you went into shock. You went into autopilot.
ALI	That's not good enough.
LEYLA	You did what you could.
ALI	Which wasn't enough. Do you think it was enough?
LEYLA	Well –
ALI	Do you think it was enough?
LEYLA	Which is why you can't take it down.
	Pause.
ALI	It could have been you.
LEYLA	I know. It could have been you.
ALI	That's what scares me.
LEYLA	It is scary. But you can't –
ALI	That people will do that. Just – Bang.
LEYLA	Yes.
ALI	Roll down a window or – Screech by on a motorbike and –
LEYLA	Cowards.

ALI   And why her?
               That's what I can't –
               What did she even do?

LEYLA   She was there.

ALI   She wasn't even *doing anything*.

LEYLA   Yes but she was there.

ALI   How is someone like that a threat?

LEYLA   Of course she's a threat.

ALI   She's just a girl in a yellow dress.

LEYLA   She was in their way.

ALI   They shouldn't just –
               How can they just *do* that?

LEYLA   Because they need to send a message.

ALI   Well.
               OK.
               Now I've sent a message.

LEYLA   You have.

ALI   So what happens now?

               Pause.

               Do you think that –
               They've seen it.

               Pause.

LEYLA   Maybe they haven't linked it to you yet.

ALI   You know I was careful.

LEYLA   I know you were.

ALI   Obviously I used a false –

LEYLA   Of course you did.

ALI   I'd never be so stupid as to –

LEYLA   No.
           I know you wouldn't.

           Pause.

           978,000 views now.

ALI   Oh.

LEYLA   979.

ALI   OK.

LEYLA   980 –

ALI   OK, stop, thanks.

           Pause.

LEYLA   I should have been there.

ALI   You were at the dentist.

LEYLA   I didn't even need a filling.
           He just said –
           Well done, I can see you've been flossing.

ALI   You would have been there otherwise.

           Pause.

LEYLA   Maybe I wouldn't.

ALI   What do you mean?

LEYLA   I mean…
           Maybe I was scared.

ALI   OK…
           No one's going to judge you for being scared.

LEYLA   Maybe they should judge me.

ALI   Why?
           You were at the dentist.

LEYLA   She wasn't scared though, was she?

ALI   Who?

LEYLA   Her.
           The girl.

ALI	She might have been…
LEYLA	No. She was there.
ALI	She – She could be anyone.
LEYLA	That's what counts, in the end. She was there.
ALI	She could be a – A lunatic. A human trafficker. A bad mother. We don't know.
LEYLA	Yes but she's visible. She matters.
ALI	You matter.
LEYLA	Hardly. I'm a chicken. A chicken with really good teeth.

Pause.

She's got good teeth.

ALI	Does she?
LEYLA	She's pretty.
ALI	Not really…
LEYLA	Come on. You know she is.

Pause.

How many times has that car been round the block?

Pause.

ALI	What car?
LEYLA	That one.

ALI The grey one?

LEYLA Yeah.

ALI I don't know.

LEYLA Quite a few.

ALI Really?

LEYLA I just noticed.

ALI Are you sure?

LEYLA Quite slowly.

ALI What do you mean?

LEYLA I mean it's going round and round quite slowly.

ALI That could be anything.
Any reason.

LEYLA Should we turn the light off?

Beat.

ALI I don't know.
Should we?

LEYLA I think we should.

ALI OK.

ALI *turns off the light.*

They wait.

LEYLA It's probably nothing.

ALI Exactly.

LEYLA Is the door locked?

ALI Uh –

LEYLA And I'm only asking because I'm being extra-careful.

ALI I don't see why it wouldn't be locked.

LEYLA We always lock it.
Why wouldn't we lock it?

ALI   I'll check if you like.

LEYLA   No.
             No need.

             Beat.

             Actually I think I might check it.

             She goes to the door.

             Checks it.

             They wait.

ALI   Leyla?

LEYLA   What?

ALI   It's Adam.

             Pause.

             It's just Adam.

LEYLA   Let me see.

             Pause.

ALI   He was just driving around looking for a parking
             spot.

LEYLA   Just Adam!

ALI   We turned the light off –

LEYLA   For Adam!

ALI   You checked the –

LEYLA   I checked the lock and everything!

ALI   Shall we just calm down, maybe?!

LEYLA   I think that's basically our only option right now.

             Beat.

ALI   OK.
             It's decided.
             I'm not taking it down.

LEYLA   Good.

ALI   This is my –
       This is my act of protest, isn't it?

LEYLA   Yes.

ALI   I don't care what they –
       I don't actually care.

LEYLA   No.

ALI   Why should I be scared of them?

LEYLA   They're scared of YOU!
         If you think about it.

ALI   They are!
       They're actually scared of ME!

LEYLA   It's like spiders.

ALI   Exactly, it's exactly like spiders.

LEYLA   'They're more scared of you than you are of them.'

ALI   They're just spiders on the toilet seat.

LEYLA   You're just going to trap them in a cup and throw
         them out the window.

ALI   Or squash them.

LEYLA   Or squash them.

ALI   Up to me.

LEYLA   It's completely up to you what you do with those
         spiders.

ALI   Let's just watch some TV and forget about it.
       For now.

       They switch on the television.

       Fuck.
       FUCK.

LEYLA   It's OK, Ali.
         Come here.

 # 5

A, B *and* C.

Perhaps they are on the television that LEYLA *and* ALI *have just switched on.*

A *steps forward.*

B *and* C *stand slightly behind, flanking her/him.*

A   Good evening.
        It is an honour to stand before you tonight.
        Tonight, with my heart full of love, I reach out to you.
        As a father reaches out towards his children.

        Pause.

        For I am not blind to current events
        These current events weigh on me heavily.
        They fill me with sadness, with compassion for the men and women who seek only to fly the flags of freedom and democracy.
        Noble, virtuous people.
        Thank you for challenging me.
        I welcome challenge.
        What I do not, and will not, welcome –
        Is chaos.

        B *hands* A *a bottle of water.*

        A *takes a swig.*

        There are some amongst you who are angry.
        Angry and, yes, afraid.
        I know this.

        And may I say how much I admire those men and women who have taken to the streets to stand up to what they see as injustice, as power at its most foul and corrupt.
        To those brave individuals I say: there is no one who detests that which is foul and corrupt as much as me.

        B *and* C *nod.*

To those brave individuals I say: I pity you.
Yes: pity.
Because you have been misled.
Misled, as so many have been misled, by the false
propaganda that seeks to destabilise the very
foundations of our society.
I pity you because you have been exploited and
manipulated by the cynical political desires
of a lunatic minority.
A ruthless, nihilistic minority comprised of
outlaws and terrorists.
But, and this is my pledge to you: I will protect
you from them.

C *taps* A *on the shoulder and whispers something
almost imperceptibly.*

A *nods.*

Turns back to audience.

In the light of recent events...
There are images that sear themselves onto our
consciousness.
There are images that horrify and appal us.
There are images that grab us by the throat and
make it hard to breathe.
But, brothers and sisters, remember: that is all
they are –
An image.
An illusion.
Pay them no more attention than you would a
small child who claims they have discovered
how to fly.

B *clears her/his throat.*

Thank you.
Thank you so much for listening to me, your
humble servant, on this most glorious night.
Goodnight.
And God bless.

6

A large house in an affluent part of West London.

NIA *and* CANDACE *are drinking tea and nibbling biscuits.*

NIA *has lots of folders in front of her.*

She has one open and is pointing at something.

NIA   This is Suli.

CANDACE   This is him?!

NIA   I'm sorry I haven't been able to get a photo until
           now –

CANDACE   Oh hello!
           Oh he's lovely.
           He's got such a *cheeky* little face!

NIA   He's certainly a handsome boy.

CANDACE   He really is.

           They look, smiling.

           NIA *turns the page.*

NIA   He drew this for you.

CANDACE   For me?

NIA   He's quite good, isn't he?
           An artist in the making, perhaps.

CANDACE   Now just a moment let me get my glasses.

           She looks for her glasses.

           Finds them and puts them on.

           Oh I say!
           Now what's this?

NIA   Well.
           This is meant to be your house.

CANDACE   Oh!
           Is that the cat?!

NIA   We told him you had a cat.
            He loves them.
            He used to have one before...

CANDACE   And that's –
            Is this supposed to be me?

NIA   He's given you a crown, look.

CANDACE   Well!
            I'm –
            Please do tell him that I'm so honoured.

NIA   You can write and tell him yourself.
            If you like?

CANDACE   Oh.
            Can I?

NIA   We encourage communication.

CANDACE   Well you see I wasn't sure –

NIA   We absolutely encourage it.

CANDACE   In that case I shall write to him this afternoon.

NIA   He'll be delighted.

CANDACE   Do you think?

NIA   The more detail the better.
            He loves detail.

CANDACE   He must be awfully clever.
            He looks clever.

NIA   Yes he's very bright, very inquisitive.

CANDACE   Oh, bless him.

NIA   Which is why everything that is happening to him
            is so...
            It is hard to take.
            I'm sure you agree.

CANDACE   How is the uh...
            How is the situation?

            Pause.

NIA   It's hard to say.
           It's volatile.

CANDACE   I've been following as much as I can on the news.

NIA   There is still no sign of his parents.

CANDACE   No?
           Nothing?

NIA   We can assume that the outcome will not be –

CANDACE   Oh no.
           Oh I can't bear it.

NIA   It is best to assume the worst.

           Pause.

           They sip tea.

           Everyone was so hopeful initially but now…

CANDACE   Sometimes I stay up half the night reading about it.

NIA   The government is cracking down.
           As predicted.

CANDACE   But it only ever seems to be that one story.

NIA   A lot of people are in prison.
           A lot of people are –

CANDACE   'The girl in the yellow dress.'

NIA   Missing.
           Dead.
           We can presume they're dead.

CANDACE   And of course I care about her.
           This poor girl.
           But you wonder about everyone else, don't you?
           It seems a shame –

NIA   Still.
           If it hadn't been for her you wouldn't have
           approached us.
           Would you?

CANDACE No.
I suppose that's true.

NIA Before her most people barely gave a second
thought to our country.

CANDACE Oh dear.
You must take a pretty dim view of the world.

NIA Not at all.
Look at everything you are doing to help.

CANDACE Ohh…

NIA Because of you we're able to help children like
Suli.
Help them get food, shelter, help them get out of
the country if needs be.
All because of people like you.

CANDACE Oh, gosh, yes, well.

Pause.

I just –
Sometimes it makes me feel a bit queasy.
All this.

She looks around the room.

It's all his, of course.
He let me keep the house.
Graciously.
And every month, thanks to his guilt, my bank
balance swells in a manner that is –
Almost obscene.

Pause.

He lives in the Norfolk property now.
With his new –
And their children.
Two girls.
They go to a Steiner school.
They call the teachers by their first names.
'Barnaby'.

And 'Debbie'.
She sends me a round robin four times a year.

She sips tea.

But I mean, goodness, *I* haven't suffered.

NIA   I'm sure it must have been painful.

CANDACE   Ohhhh.
                 Not compared to you.

NIA   It's relative.
                 Everything is.

CANDACE   I mean, sometimes, at night…
                 Sleeping isn't my greatest skill, put it that way.
                 Ha!

NIA   Knitting helps, I find.

CANDACE   Oh really?
                 I'm all fingers and thumbs sadly.

NIA   Better to get up and do something than lie there
                 and fester.

CANDACE   You have trouble sleeping?

NIA   Oh I'm a –
                 Seasoned insomniac.

CANDACE   I tend to have the World Service on all night.

NIA   Ah yes.

CANDACE   But it can be rather dampening.
                 I mean, there's so much one is so powerless to
                 control.

NIA   Yes.

CANDACE   So many horrors.

NIA   That's true.

CANDACE   Sometimes I think, well Candace, you don't
                 deserve to sleep.

                 Pause.

So I try to help.
I want to help.
Is it helpful?
I don't know.
Money...
It makes me feel rather empty that all I can offer is money.

NIA   It makes a huge difference.

CANDACE   Yes but it's –
I don't know.
It's remote, isn't it?

NIA   Not for Suli.
Not for all those children.

CANDACE   Yes.
Yes thank goodness I can help them...

They sip tea.

NIA *opens another folder, thumbs through it.*

Opens it on a page and shows it to CANDACE.

NIA   This is my father.
My mother.

CANDACE   Oh aren't they elegant!

NIA   This is their wedding day.

CANDACE   Doesn't she have *lovely* eyes?

NIA   They were both journalists.
Very smart, very well-educated.

CANDACE   You've got her eyes, haven't you, Nia?

NIA   They opposed the regime.
Vehemently.
And vocally.

NIA *turns the page.*

This is what happened to them.

CANDACE   Oh –

CANDACE looks away and puts her hand over her face.

Silence.

NIA closes the folder.

NIA   The death certificates, when eventually they were made available –
Gave 'meningitis' as the cause of death.

Pause.

I grew up with a small asterix next to my name.
Which ensured I couldn't be admitted to university.
Or gain employment of any meaningful kind.
I was often arrested, on the smallest pretext.

She rolls back the sleeves of her top.

They did this to me.

CANDACE looks at NIA's wrists.

Swallows.

With a broken bottle.
They sawed it back and forth over my wrist.

CANDACE   Why did they do that?

NIA   I was kept in solitary confinement for several months.

CANDACE   Oh...

NIA   Assaulted, sexually.

CANDACE   No.

NIA   I was released, arrested again, released...
The cycle continued...

CANDACE   How...
Awful.

NIA   Until eventually I was able to escape.
            Smuggled out of the country in the boot of a car.
            That was fourteen years ago.

            NIA *rolls down her sleeve again.*

            You must never underestimate what money does.
            Never.

            Pause.

            You'll find we all have a –
            A deeply personal investment in this cause.

CANDACE Yes.

NIA   You will meet all of us, I hope.
            We're very social.
            We've created a kind of network.
            Parties, dinners, symposiums.
            I think you'll enjoy the interaction.

CANDACE Yes.

NIA   Perhaps you might consider hosting something
            yourself.

CANDACE Here?

NIA   You have a beautiful home.

            Beat.

CANDACE I should love to.

NIA   And many friends, no doubt.
            People, like you, who –
            Who bristle at the injustices of the world.

CANDACE Well I hope so.
            I hope they do –

NIA   It's so important to raise awareness.
            It is imperative that people know.
            It is vital that –
            That the world doesn't forget what is happening
            there.

CANDACE   I agree.
    I really do.

NIA   Perhaps we could look at three weeks' time.
    Does that sounds good?

CANDACE   Oh.
    Um –

NIA   Is that enough time?

CANDACE   Uh –
    Yes.
    Of course.

NIA   If you're quite sure?

CANDACE   No, yes, I'll put some invitations together and
    send them out this week.
    It won't be any trouble.

NIA   I can draft the invitations.

CANDACE   Ah.
    Yes?

NIA   Just to ensure the tone is correct.

CANDACE   Of course.
    I quite understand.

    NIA *begins to gather up her folders.*

    Is time up?

NIA   I've got another appointment.
    Thank you so much for the delicious tea.

CANDACE   Did you like it?
    It's Fortnum and Mason's own blend.
    Someone got me one of those hampers at
    Christmas.

NIA   I must get some.

CANDACE   Do you need a cab?
    I can call you one.

NIA   No.
           It's very close.
           I can walk.

CANDACE   And you'll come again?

NIA   Oh yes.
           Of course.

CANDACE   Well.
           You're always welcome.
           I've very much enjoyed meeting you face to face.
           It's been –
           Well I've certainly –
           Thank you.

           NIA *reaches out to shake* CANDACE*'s hand.*

NIA   I'll be in touch.

7

A, B *and* C *enter, with yellow fabric around their wrists.*

C *is wearing a yellow dress.*

They all have yellow balloons.

YASMIN – *a little grubbier than before – is unable to get past*
A, B *and* C.

A   Please, take a balloon.

B   A balloon for you?

C   Madam, a balloon?

YASMIN   (*Trying to get through.*) Excuse me.
           Sorry.
           Can I get through?

B   Has everyone got one?

C   Stick your hands up if you haven't got one.

B   Is everyone taking pictures?
             Please, please take as many pictures as you can.

A   Yes, please, it's really important.
             We need total saturation.

B   We need this to be the front page of every
             newspaper in every country.

A   We need to show that we're not cowed.
             That we'll never give up!

B   That they can't intimidate us with their truncheons
             and their helmets and their guns!

YASMIN   (*To* C.) Can you let me through?

C   (*Handing her a balloon.*) Here you go.

             YASMIN *looks at the balloon in her hand.*

YASMIN   What's this for?

C   She might be about to wake up.

YASMIN   Who?
             Listen, I need to get inside the hospital –

C   That's her room.
             That one right at the top, to the left.

B   There's going to be a minute of silence in her
             honour.

A   And then we'll each release our balloon, into the
             air, at the same time.
             As a tribute to her.

C   Imagine if she looked down.
             And she saw all of us.

YASMIN   Are they not letting people in?

C   Imagine if she could see how much people love her.

YASMIN   It's just I badly need to get inside.

C   Are you hurt?

YASMIN   No –

C   Have those bastards hurt you?

YASMIN   No, no, it's nothing like that.
          I'm just –

C   Show me what they've done to you.

YASMIN   I'm looking for my mother.

C   You look shattered, you poor thing.

YASMIN   Well I –
          Do I?
          I haven't really slept, much.

C   It's hard to sleep, isn't it?
          With those monsters out there.
          They mow people down, you know.

YASMIN   Sorry?

C   With horses.
          With tanks.

YASMIN   They –
          What?

C   We're just insects to them.

YASMIN   No.
          She was just shopping.
          She was just –

C   Who?

YASMIN   My mum.

C   They've got your mum?

YASMIN   No!
          Nothing like that!

B   OK, it's a bit of a scrum so let's just –

A   Try not to push.
          There's no need to push.

YASMIN   What were you saying though?
            About –
            Mowing people down?

C   You can't dwell on it.
            You can't let it scare you.

YASMIN   No but –
            That sounds bad…

A   God there's so many people…

B   (*To* A.) Are you OK?

A   I need some air…

B   Don't stop, you've got to keep going.

C   Can everyone stop pushing?

YASMIN   But I mean, she had her crappy old straw hat on!
            Why would they do that to her?

C   I said, don't push!

YASMIN   And she's tough, that's the thing.
            I mean, she's not the kind of person you mess
            with.
            I've got a picture if you want to keep your eyes
            peeled –

C   Look!

YASMIN   What?

C   She's –
            The curtains they're…!

A   Is it?

B   Do you think it's…?

C   Is it her?
            Is it actually her?

A   Wait!
            Don't let go yet.
            Please just wait –

YASMIN   Hello?

C   Is it her?

B   Is it – ?

Pause.

They all hold their breath.

Then collectively let it out again.

C   What was that you were saying?
     What's that you've got?

YASMIN *looks at the crumpled piece of paper in
her hand.*

She crumples it up even more.

YASMIN   Nothing.
          Never mind.

 # 8

A café.

Evening.

LEYLA *and* ALI *sit silently at a table together.*

A and B *are sitting, separately, at two more tables.*

Silence.

LEYLA   Well this is nice.

ALI   Yeah.

LEYLA   I'm not sure we've managed more than ten words
         between us but –
         Yes.
         Nice to get out.

ALI   Ha!
       Right.

ALI *looks nervously around and behind him.*

LEYLA   I even waxed my legs.

             She sticks her leg out for him to admire.

             He pats it absent-mindedly.

             Your raw lust is dizzying.

ALI   Look I did something I kind of regret.

LEYLA   Right.

ALI   I spoke to this –
             This like blog thing.

LEYLA   OK.
             Right.
             What –

             C approaches with a pad.

C   Ready to order?

LEYLA   Ummm.

C   I'm afraid we don't have any soup left.
             Oh and only vegetarian options on the
             sandwiches.
             We're clean out of meat.

ALI   Uh –

LEYLA   I don't know, some tea?

ALI   Yeah tea, tea's fine.

C   Tea?

LEYLA   Yes please.

C   Tea…

             C writes it down slowly.

             They wait for C to leave.

             C smiles.

	We haven't had a delivery in I don't know how many days now. When will all this nonsense be over, that's what I want to know?
LEYLA	Mm.
ALI	Mm.
C	I don't know, I just think it's all bonkers, I honestly do!

C twiddles her/his hair and smiles a bit more.

Anyway, you'll yell if you need me?

C saunters away.

LEYLA *and* ALI *speak quietly.*

LEYLA	What blog?
ALI	I don't know, something in New York. Zane works there.
LEYLA	So he knows to keep you anonymous.
ALI	He got in touch, like, 'do you know anything about this girl?!' And I sort of had to say – Yes.
LEYLA	He'll make sure it's safe. He's your friend.
ALI	I haven't seen him for what? Five years?
LEYLA	You keep in touch.
ALI	So you think I can trust him?
LEYLA	Um. Well, it's not really him we've got to worry about, is it?
ALI	So you think I've made a massive mistake?
LEYLA	Maybe you should have wrestled with this yourself before blurting everything out but –

ALI   This is Zane we're talking about.
              Zane!

LEYLA   Yes.
              I got that.

ALI   I'm not a complete idiot.

LEYLA   We said we weren't going to talk about it tonight.
              Remember?

              Pause.

ALI   Sorry.
              Am I being a nightmare?

LEYLA   A little bit.
              But I forgive you.
              As long as you dazzle me with your scintillating
              conversation for the rest of the night.

ALI   Thing is, he said something else.

LEYLA   Nope.
              Not dazzling enough, sorry.

ALI   He said that, if he was me…
              He'd be scared.

              Pause.

              He could help us, you see.
              With paperwork and stuff.
              He said he knows people.

LEYLA   Sorry –
              What paperwork?

ALI   You know.
              If we wanted to –
              To go there.

LEYLA   To New York?

ALI   Yeah.
              Yes.

              Beat.

LEYLA	Is this – Are you serious?
ALI	Yes.
LEYLA	Why? What's happened?
ALI	Nothing.
LEYLA	You have to tell me if – If –
ALI	Nothing's happened. I promise.

Beat.

But you don't think it's weird?

LEYLA	Think what's weird?
ALI	This… silence?

Silence.

B *approaches.*

B	Are you finished with that?
LEYLA	What?
B	Your newspaper.
LEYLA	Have it.

B *takes the newspaper.*

Opens it.

Shakes head.

B	Extraordinary…

They wait for B to leave.

B *wanders back to table.*

LEYLA *and* ALI *resume speaking, at an even quieter volume.*

ALI	Can we talk about it?

LEYLA   What?
           About New York?

ALI   Yes.

LEYLA   So, just up sticks in the middle of all of this?
           Take a jaunt up the Empire State Building?

ALI   No –

LEYLA   Sorry guys!
           You're all standing up for freedom and risking
           your lives or whatever.
           We're buying Basquiat postcards in the MOMA
           gift shop!

ALI   Please.
           Let's talk about it.
           Seriously.

           A *gets up and moves her/his chair a bit closer to*
           ALI *and* LEYLA.

A   Don't mind me!
           Better light over here.

           A *smiles*.

           ALI *and* LEYLA *resume at a quieter volume*.

LEYLA   Right.
           Seriously.
           Where would we work?

ALI   Uh –
           Well, Zane would help us get something.

LEYLA   What kind of thing?

ALI   Um –

LEYLA   Where would we live?

ALI   I, I guess…
           Someone's sofa for a bit until – ?

LEYLA   Would my parents come with us?

ALI   What?

LEYLA   Would they?

ALI   Well…
         That's probably not realistic.

         Pause.

LEYLA   OK.

ALI   Obviously we couldn't…
         I mean that's a whole other…

         Pause.

         What do you want me to say?

LEYLA   I'm not sure.

         Pause.

ALI   You could call them.
         Your family.
         You could call them every day.

LEYLA   Oh.

ALI   People do it.
         They do it all the time.

LEYLA   Yeah.

ALI   People in much worse situations than ours.
         We're lucky.

LEYLA   Oh right.

ALI   We know people.
         People who can help us and, and make it as
         bearable as it can be.
         Loads of people don't have that option –

LEYLA   How are we funding this?

ALI   Sorry?

LEYLA   How are we funding it?
         This complex operation.

         Pause.

ALI	We'll… we'll scrape it together.
LEYLA	I can't imagine it comes cheap.
ALI	We'll manage.
LEYLA	Or we could just ask my uncle.
	Pause.
ALI	Well, no, but… We couldn't…
LEYLA	He's filthy rich. Isn't he?
ALI	Well yeah but… It didn't occur to me that we would –
LEYLA	It didn't? Are you sure?
ALI	Yes.
LEYLA	He's rolling in cash. You've said it yourself a million times.
ALI	I know but –
LEYLA	Rolling around in all that dodgy cash. Like a big, smug sea lion, I think is how you described it.
ALI	I don't think I put it quite –
LEYLA	You've always had a lot to say about my uncle.
ALI	Yeah but I was being an idiot. I was just being a judgemental prick. I mean, what do I know about his life?
LEYLA	Oh, now you understand him? That's great! I'm so pleased you've finally found it in your heart to forgive him –
ALI	Hey –

LEYLA   Now that he's able to buy your safety with all that
           garish gold you hate so much.
           He'll be so happy!

           Pause.

ALI   I wasn't assuming –
           Leyla, I wasn't.

LEYLA   Five minutes ago I knew where I was.
           And suddenly I'm, I'm breaking my mum's heart,
           I'm bleeding my uncle dry and I'm
           smuggling myself inside a Fedex box.

           C *returns with tea.*

C   Shall I just – ?

ALI   Just put it down.

LEYLA   We can manage.

C   I'm alright just to – ?

ALI   Yes.

LEYLA   Yes.

C   You'll give me a nod if you need anything else?

ALI   Yes!

           C *retreats.*

           Pause.

           Or I could just go.

LEYLA   What?

           C *returns.*

C   Did you want sugar?

ALI   No.

C   (*To* LEYLA.) What about you?

LEYLA   No.

C   If you want any you'll just holler?

LEYLA	Yes.
	C retreats.
	What did you just say?
ALI	I could go. On my own.
	A sneezes loudly.
A	Oof. Excuse me.
LEYLA	OK. Now this feels like a whole other conversation.
ALI	You're right. You shouldn't have to leave your family, your home. I wouldn't make you do that.
LEYLA	You go? On your own?
ALI	I don't want to drag you into my mess.
LEYLA	Hang on. I thought it was our mess.
ALI	I'm the one who made the film.
LEYLA	I'm the one who told you to put it up.
ALI	They don't have to know that.
LEYLA	OK. Right.
	She takes a long slurp of her tea then spits it out.
	Fuck!
ALI	Hot?
LEYLA	Fucking *scalding*!
	Pause.
	Something occurred to me actually.
ALI	Yeah?

LEYLA   That day.
          The day of the –

ALI   Yes?

LEYLA   You were filming her before she got shot.
          Before.

          Beat.

ALI   Yeah.

LEYLA   How come?

ALI   What do you mean?

LEYLA   How come you were filming her?

ALI   I don't really know.
          That's just the way it was.

LEYLA   Did you know her?

ALI   No.

          Pause.

LEYLA   So she just caught your eye.

ALI   Well –
          I guess she did.

LEYLA   The dress, probably.

ALI   Uh.
          Yeah maybe.

LEYLA   What with it being so bright.

ALI   I expect so.

LEYLA   That's probably it.

          Pause.

          OK.
          I'll speak to my uncle.

ALI   You don't have to.

LEYLA   If you think this is the only way then, then OK.

          Pause.

Then it's decided.
I'll go and see him tomorrow.

Pause.

ALI   Thank you.
           I mean it.
           And I'm sorry.

LEYLA   Yeah.
           I know you are.

 # 9

CANDACE *and* NIA.

CANDACE*'s house.*

Night-time.

They are drying glasses.

Silence.

CANDACE   Well, I think that went well.

NIA   You spoke brilliantly.

CANDACE   Did I?

NIA   You really communicated something, I think.

CANDACE   Oh I do hope so.

NIA   Your passion.

CANDACE   People seemed interested, didn't they?

NIA   I spoke to lots of very kind people.

CANDACE   And they seemed – ?

NIA   The main thing is to plant a seed.
           No one wants to be forced.
           That's not how we operate.

CANDACE   Well I hope it yields something for you.
            I really do.
            Gosh, I'm done in!

            Pause.

            NIA *continues to shine glasses.*

            The cleaning lady's actually coming in the
            morning.

NIA   It's no trouble.

CANDACE   You'll be wanting to get home.

NIA   The bus goes all night.

CANDACE   Oh you can't get the bus!

NIA   I like the bus.

CANDACE   Are you sure you don't want me to call you a cab?

NIA   I'll be perfectly fine on the bus.

            Pause.

CANDACE   Anyway.

            Pause.

            I wonder if you spoke to my friend, Miles.
            You might have spotted him.
            Tall, rather leonine.
            Noble-looking, I've always thought.
            He certainly thinks so!

NIA   The barrister.

CANDACE   That's him.

NIA   Lovely voice.

CANDACE   Oh that's Eton for you.
            Anyway he's a very old pal.
            Used to be married to my friend Evelyn.
            My best friend, I suppose you'd say.
            Anyway, she died.
            Few years ago now.

Ovarian cancer.
Quite ghastly.

NIA   I'm so sorry.

CANDACE   Yes.
             She was fun.
             She was great fun.

NIA   That must be hard.
             For both of you.

CANDACE   Yes we miss her.
             Horribly…
             But we soldier on.
             Well.
             As you'll know.

             Beat.

             Anyway he mentioned –
             I was just chatting to him all about you and what
             you do, and he was full of admiration, of course.

NIA   Where do these go?

CANDACE   What?
             Oh, that cupboard behind you.
             Anyway –

NIA   This one?

CANDACE   Yes.
             Anyway he –
             The thing is he mentioned –
             He said he'd done a bit of digging.
             He's completely *obsessed* with the internet and the
             problem is he has a tendency to sort of believe
             absolutely everything he reads.
             I've told him so many times, I've said, Miles, half
             of it is utter nonsense, it really is!
             But he's stubborn and anyway the thing is he said
             that he'd stumbled across a few things that he just
             wanted to um –
             Well, flag up to me, I suppose.

             Pause.

Obviously you do all that wonderful work for
those children.
And obviously you're opposed to the government
that –
That inflicts such unutterable misery.
Which is completely understandable.

Pause.

But he just mentioned a few things to me about
well –
Oh dear.
Methods.
Particular methods.

Pause.

Violence.

Pause.

Bombs.

Pause.

And I said –
I said, that can't possibly be true.
This is a reputable charity!
I trust them.
I inherently trust them and deeply believe in
everything they do.

Pause.

But he said that perhaps I should just
double-check.
Where it is the money –
My money –
Actually, well, *goes.*

NIA *slowly finishes shining a glass.*

NIA   You would like to see our accounts?

Pause.

Very well.
Of course.

CANDACE   Perhaps I could get Miles round and all three of us
          could...
          I don't know!
          Stop his silly flapping!

NIA   I can bring them round next time, if you wish.
          If you'd like to check.

          NIA *starts putting on her coat*.

CANDACE   Oh dear.
          You see, now I feel like a policeman.

NIA   It's perfectly understandable.
          You have been generous.
          Extremely generous.
          You want to know precisely where it is that your
          money goes.

CANDACE   Well he's always been a bit paranoid to be honest.
          Used to drive Evelyn utterly bananas.
          He was swindled by Lloyds so his antenna is
          rather 'up' when it comes to anything financial.

NIA   It's no trouble.
          I'll gather the relevant information and we can go
          through it together.
          If that is what you need.
          I am happy to reassure you.

CANDACE   Oh dear I don't need reassurance.
          It's just Miles.
          It's honestly just –

NIA   I'll call this week.

          Pause.

CANDACE   I –
          I haven't offended you, have I?

NIA   Not in the slightest.

CANDACE   I do hope I haven't.

NIA   But I need to be sure I have a commitment from
          you.
          For Suli's sake.

CANDACE   I'm, I'm committed.
          I promise.

NIA   Because abandonment at this stage would be
          very –
          Damaging.
          And if abandonment is a possibility then I need to
          rethink my position, with regards our
          relationship.

CANDACE   You don't need to.
          Honestly.
          I'm –
          I would never abandon Suli.

          Pause.

NIA   Thank you for a very successful evening.
          I'll see myself out.

CANDACE   Wait!

          Pause.

          I just don't want to be out of my depth.

NIA   That's entirely up to you.
          Goodbye.

 # 10

A *picks up a microphone.*

B *has a video camera.*

YASMIN – *tired, dirty, sleep-deprived – watches them.*

A   So, it's tense on the streets today as you can
                 probably see.
                 People aren't quite sure where's safe and where
                 isn't and there's quite a bit of confusion and
                 general uneasiness.
                 We've been hearing heavy gunfire and there's
                 been lots of shouting and there are reports
                 that there have been some, uh, possibly some
                 fatalities but I should emphasise that these
                 are, at present, unconfirmed.

                 B *gets a phone call.*

B   Yeah?

A   The protesters are grimly clinging on, as you can
                 see.
                 But I've spoken to several who say that they're
                 beginning to lose faith even as their anger mounts.
                 The government's response is characteristically
                 heavy-handed and, even in moments of calm like
                 this, there's a sense that violence won't be far
                 behind –

B   OK.
                 Shit.
                 Sorry, we have to move on.

A   What?

B   I don't know.
                 They're just saying we have to go back to the hotel.

A   Fuck.

B   We've got to pack up and get out of here.

YASMIN   BBC?

A   Great.
           First they cut short our trip and now they're
           dictating to us when we can and can't film.

YASMIN   Excuse me?
           BBC.

           A glances at YASMIN.

A   Can you…?
           I don't understand what she's –
           Can we get her out of the way?

YASMIN   Yes?
           BBC?

B   Uh…

A   Just tell her we're BBC if it'll make her happy.

B   (*To* YASMIN.) Yes.
           Yes, BBC!

           YASMIN *waves the picture excitedly.*

           Uhhhh…?

YASMIN   You, um…?

           She waves the picture.

B   Some woman with a scar…

           YASMIN *points to the camera.*

           She points to her mouth.

           We could give her a few minutes.
           Sort of a human-interest thing.

A   No offence but she's not really the angle we're
           going for.

B   (*To* YASMIN.) Um, you want to – ?
           On the – ?

           YASMIN *nods.*

A   What are you doing?

B   You know, I'm just concerned we're not getting
           that well-rounded a picture.
           We just keep talking to college kids with good
           haircuts and expensive shoes.

A   You're the one who just said we had to leave!

B   (*To* YASMIN.) OK, I'm going to point this at you
           and –

           B *trains the camera on* YASMIN*'s face.*

           YASMIN *holds out the picture.*

           *She delivers the following speech – the first few
           lines are spoken backwards to give the impression
           that* YASMIN *is speaking a foreign language. The
           actor can deliver the whole speech backwards if
           she likes, otherwise the rest can be spoken as it is
           written.*

YASMIN   Esaelp.
           I dlouw ekil enoyreve ot wonk taht siht si ym
           rehtom, dna taht ehs si gnissim.
           I tnevah nees reh, ro draeh morf reh, ni rouf syad.

           Please.
           I would like everyone to know that this is my
           mother, and that she is missing.
           I haven't seen her, or heard from her, in four days.
           Her name's Marion, she's fifty-five and she's got
           this scar, here, as you can see, because a dog bit
           her a few years ago when she tried to give him
           some scraps.
           I'm not sure who's watching this and what good it
           does me saying all this and I'm not a very
           articulate person anyway but I suppose I'm just
           hoping that the more people see this, the more
           chance there is that I'll –
           That I'll find her.
           Soon, I hope.

A   In case you'd forgotten, our translator got arrested.

YASMIN   And also to say that if she's watching this then I'd
            be really grateful if she could call me or, or
            find some way of getting in touch with me.
            I'm sure she wants to but obviously something
            very unusual has happened and I...
            There's a lot of... it's a very unpredictable time, it
            feels like quite a violent time and I would
            hate for her to...

            They watch her in incomprehension.

A   (*To* B.) Stop filming.
            I said stop filming.

B   She's still speaking.

A   It's OK.
            We won't tell her we've stopped.
            She can get it out of her system.

            B *hesitates, then stops filming – but keeps the
            camera trained on* YASMIN*'s face.*

YASMIN   Please tell everyone. I know I'm not the only
            person this is happening to but...
            I know I'm just a tiny person in the middle of
            something huge but –

A   OK.
            OK, THANK YOU!
            That's great.
            REALLY great.

            YASMIN *recognises the finality of her/his tone.*

            She lowers the picture.

            Nods.

YASMIN   Everyone.

            She gestures – 'the whole world'.

            Everywhere.

A   Yep.
            Yep, absolutely.

YASMIN   Thank you.

A   Don't mention it.

YASMIN   Thank you.
           Thank you.

11

LEYLA *and* ALI*'s apartment.*

LEYLA*, alone.*

She sits very still.

ALI *enters.*

ALI   There's no bread anywhere.
           I could only get these cracker things and I had to
           walk about three miles –

           He notices LEYLA.

           Leyla?
           You alright?

           Pause.

           Leyla?

LEYLA   You said you didn't know her.

ALI   What?

LEYLA   The girl.

           Pause.

           'Never seen her before in my life.'
           That's what you said.

           Silence.

ALI   OK.
           OK I knew her a little bit.

LEYLA	Yes.
ALI	Hardly at all.
LEYLA	Right.
ALI	We did classes in the same building and I – I saw her a few times.
LEYLA	Saw her.
ALI	Yes.
LEYLA	Right.
ALI	OK we spoke a few times.
LEYLA	Yes.
ALI	Which isn't a crime! Is, is speaking to another girl a crime?
LEYLA	Not as far as I know. No.
	Pause.
ALI	The only reason I didn't tell you is – Is cos I didn't want you to get the wrong idea.
LEYLA	OK.
ALI	Because there isn't anything. There's nothing! Honestly Leyla there's –
LEYLA	I went on your computer.
ALI	Um. What?
LEYLA	Yes.
ALI	Why – Why would you go on my computer?
LEYLA	A whole folder.
ALI	You can't just – Hack into someone's computer, that's –
LEYLA	A whole folder devoted to her.

ALI   No.
               Hang on.
               Hang on let's just think about who's got the moral
               high ground here.

LEYLA   Your new muse.

ALI   If you want to know something, Leyla, you should
               just confront me.
               You shouldn't go rooting around in someone's
               personal –

LEYLA   It wasn't me.

ALI   What?

LEYLA   It was the men.

ALI   What men?

LEYLA   The men who were here earlier.

               Pause.

               The men who did this to the apartment.

               ALI *looks around and realises the flat is in
               disarray.*

               Pause.

               They found your computer and they opened it and
               it took them about five seconds.

               Pause.

               They said, you're very beautiful.
               No wonder your boyfriend has all these pictures
               and films of you.

               Pause.

               I said, that's not me.
               That's the girl who's nearly dead in hospital.
               The girl you shot.
               They smiled.

               Pause.

They said, you're an actress, right?
A porn actress.

Pause.

And your boyfriend.
He makes porn films.

Pause.

They said, why would you make this film?

Pause.

This film, where you writhe so provocatively and
reveal your underwear to the world.

Pause.

They said, obviously you made this film to
discredit us.

Pause.

They said, why don't you go on television, tell
everyone it was just an illusion.
Just a story.

Pause.

Because there is no girl, lying in a hospital bed,
with a tube coming out of her nose.
She doesn't exist.
Does she?

Pause.

Then one of them put his truncheon under my skirt
and lifted it.

Pause.

So I said, no she doesn't.

Pause.

You're right.
It was me.
Me and my boyfriend made the film together.

Pause.

That was very silly and very rash, they said.
I agreed with them.

Pause.

But we're prepared to be lenient, they said.
The one with the truncheon pushed it up a little
further.

Pause.

Because you're going to do a statement, aren't
you?
You and your boyfriend.
That's what you're going to do.

Pause.

I agreed with them.

Pause.

No one got shot, did they?
I agreed with them.
And you're going to tell everyone?
I agreed with them.
And you're going to kiss this nice man now,
aren't you?
I agreed with them.

Silence.

After a while ALI *puts his head in his hands.*

We're expected at the Broadcasting Centre
tomorrow at nine.

She starts to leave.

ALI   Where are you going?

LEYLA   For a walk.

Pause.

I'll be back in half an hour.
An hour.
I don't know.

ALI   Leyla –

             She's gone.

12

The hospital waiting room.

The sound of wailing.

A *is sitting in front of a computer.*

YASMIN – *even more sleep-deprived, hot and sweaty – has just given* A *the photo.*

A   What is this?

YASMIN   It's my mum.

A   Yes?

YASMIN   I need to find out if she's here.

A   Right.
             Name?

YASMIN   Her name or my – ?

A   Her name.

YASMIN   Marion –

A   CAN SOMEONE TELL ME WHY THIS
             SCREEN KEEPS FREEZING?

             C *enters with a tray of implements and pushes
             past* YASMIN.

C   Excuse me.
             Out the way!

YASMIN   Sorry –

C   No, not in there!
             STRICTLY prohibited.

YASMIN   OK I'm sorry.

C   For goodness' sake.
             Be *careful*.

A   I can't do my job if even the simplest technology
             is going to fail me EVERY time.

             C *exits*.

YASMIN   (*To* A.) Is it true what they're saying?
             About all those people?
             Under those –
             Those big government cars?
             Their faces all…
             Is that really true?

             A*'s phone rings*.

A   (*Into phone*.) Yes?

             A *sighs*.

             Just a moment.
             Yes I said just a *moment*.

             A *taps into the computer*.

YASMIN   Can you tell that caller to wait?

A   (*Into phone*.) I tried to explain to you before,
             madam.
             He was taken to the morgue this morning.
             Yes, that's what I said.

             A *holds the phone away from her/his ear*.

YASMIN   I was in the middle of talking to you.
             We'd started a conversation.

A   (*Into phone*.) All I have is the information in the
             computer in front of me.
             I need to ask you to keep calm.
             I know.
             I know and I'm sorry –

YASMIN   I'm at the front of the queue.
             It's my turn.

A   (*To* YASMIN.) Do you think you're the only
           person here?

YASMIN   You can't just –
           Act as if it isn't my turn.

A   Do you think you're the only person with a
           missing mother?
           Or a missing eye or a missing arm?
           Do you think you're more important?

YASMIN   I've been waiting since this morning.
           Hours and hours and hours.

A   People come in here with their fingers in plastic
           bags.
           Did you know that?

YASMIN   I'll chop mine off if that's what it takes.

           *She seizes a pair of scissors from a tray and holds
           them up.*

           If that's what's required, then that's what I'll do.
           I'm so sick of people telling me to get out the way
           or to wait my turn or, or, or to take a balloon.
           Cos unless that balloon has a tiny mini-version of
           my mum inside it I'm not interested, OK?

A   OK.
           Security?

           B approaches YASMIN.

           B has a cloth clamped to her/his head.

B   Are you a nurse?

YASMIN   No.

B   Now listen.
           I think I've been shot.
           I think there's a bullet and I think it's in my head.
           I'm scared that if I take this cloth off my head that
           it will all just –
           Flop open.

YASMIN   Can someone – ?
             I think this man needs some help?

B   Like my head is in segments like an orange and
             this cloth is the only thing keeping the segments
             together.

A   I need you to take a seat over there, sir.
             SIR.

             B *starts to unwrap the bandage.*

B   Could you just give it a glance and tell me how
             bad it is?

A   And can someone get that woman OUT of here?

             C *enters carrying bedding.*

             YASMIN *pushes past* B.

B   Hey, where do you think you're going?

             YASMIN *intercepts* C.

YASMIN   Hi.
             Hello.

             YASMIN *bars her way.*

C   Excuse me.

YASMIN   Nope.
             Not moving.

C   Can someone get this woman out of my way?

YASMIN   Listen to me.
             I'm very tired.
             I'm very dizzy cos I haven't eaten for two days
             straight.

C   Alright.
             Let's just calm down –

YASMIN   I've been to every hospital in the city.
             I've waited in lines.
             I've fallen asleep in waiting-room chairs.

I've got blisters all over my feet and my shoes are full of blood.

C   I'll be able to help you in five minutes –

YASMIN   No.
           Not five minutes.
           Now.

C   You're going to have to be a little bit patient.

YASMIN   No.

C   Just let me change this bedding and I'll be with you in five –

YASMIN   No I can't let you.
           I can't, I can't, I can't, I can't, I can't, I can't, I can't…

           She runs out of words.

           She stumbles.

           C *catches her.*

           Please.
           Look at it.
           Look at her.
           Please.

           Slowly C *takes the piece of paper and studies it.*

C   Who is this, love?

YASMIN   My mother.
           Her name's Marion.

           Pause.

           It's the thought that she might think I'm not looking for her.
           That I don't care.
           That's what's killing me.

           Pause.

C   I… I think I might have…

YASMIN   You… you actually recognise her?

          YASMIN throws her arms around C.

          After a while you start to think you're going mad
          or something!

          *C allows him/herself to be hugged for a moment
          then gently disentangles from YASMIN.*

          Why are you looking at me like that?

          Pause.

C   You might want to try the coroner's office.

YASMIN   Who?

C   The coroner, sweetheart.

YASMIN   What do you mean the coroner?

C   I'm –
          I'm sorry, love.

YASMIN   Why are you sorry?
          What do you mean?

          *B approaches YASMIN again and tugs at her
          arm.*

B   How bad is it?
          Please can you tell me?

C   (*To* YASMIN.) I'm sorry.
          I've got to get on.

          C moves away from YASMIN.

B   TELL me.

YASMIN   There's nothing there, you stupid idiot.

B   I –
          I've been shot!

YASMIN   No you haven't.

B   I can feel it in there!

A   Sir!
           I really need to ask you to sit down and wait your
           turn.

B   You're a disgrace to your profession.
           Call yourself a nurse?
           You can't even be bothered to brush your hair?!
           WHORE.

           YASMIN *exits*.

 # 13

CANDACE, *alone, late at night.*

She is drinking a solitary glass of wine.

Listening to the World Service.

Her phone rings – an unknown number.

She tuts and lets it ring out.

A few moments later it starts ringing again.

She tuts again and picks it up.

CANDACE   Yes?

           Silence.

           Well if you're not going to say anything then I'm
           going to hang up.
           Goodbye.

           *A strange sound can be heard, tinnily, from the
           phone.*

           A sort of gasping and sighing.

           It could possibly be sexual.

           CANDACE *shifts uncomfortably.*

The noise resolves itself into the sound of someone in intense pain.

They are screaming and begging in a language CANDACE *can't understand.*

She drops the phone hastily.

The sound continues.

She stares at the phone.

Eventually and abruptly it goes dead.

CANDACE *continues to stare at her phone.*

Gingerly she picks it up.

She is about to switch it off when it rings again.

She answers it.

NIA   What you just heard, Candace.
Is happening now.
Right now.
He is a young man.
Only twenty.
He has dark-brown hair and a gap between his front teeth.

Pause.

His fingernails are being slowly removed.
When they have finished with his fingernails they will begin on his fingers.
They will remove them, one by one, knuckle by knuckle, with a jagged knife.
It will take a long time, and it will be very painful.

Pause.

CANDACE   Why –
Why are you telling me this?

Pause.

NIA   Because this is happening.
It is happening.

CANDACE   I don't know what to –
                      What do you want me to – ?

NIA   You must know how grateful we are, Candace.
                      You are such a good friend to us.
                      To Suli.

                      Pause.

                      Friends don't judge one another.
                      Friends don't leave any room for doubt.
                      Friends don't tiptoe away when things get messy,
                      or frightening –

CANDACE   But I –
                      I haven't tiptoed away.
                      I promise –

NIA   There is still so much that has to happen, Candace.

CANDACE   Yes.

NIA   And I have to be sure that you're aware of that.

CANDACE   But I am.
                      All those poor children –

NIA   It isn't just children, Candace.

CANDACE   No.

NIA   It's a whole, a whole *nation*.
                      A whole nation suffering.
                      A whole nation persecuted.

CANDACE   Yes.

NIA   It needs to be completely ripped up.
                      It needs to start again.

CANDACE   Yes.

NIA   And when you rip something up –
                      It might not always be –
                      Palatable.

CANDACE   No.

NIA   It can't always be a girl in a yellow dress.
            A girl who does nothing but rather, something *is
            done to her.*
            Do you think there would even be a video,
            Candace, if she wasn't so completely passive?

CANDACE   I, I don't know –

NIA   If she was dressed all in black, with teeth missing,
            holding a Kalashnikov?
            Would there have been a video then?
            What if she was holding up a nail bomb and
            spitting?
            Her hair falling out in clumps, her skin
            pockmarked?
            What if there was blood and scalp and flesh
            beneath her nails?
            Actual human flesh.

CANDACE   I don't know –

NIA   Would he have trained his camera on her then?
            Or would he just have turned and run.
            And never looked back?

            Pause.

            Sometimes it can't be peaceful.
            Because we don't feel peaceful.
            Sometimes we want to turn on the man who has
            systematically beaten and abused us.
            We want to put explosives in the kitchens of the
            restaurants he dines in, in the urinals he pisses into.
            We want to rip him to pieces.
            We want to leave him disfigured and maimed on
            the courtroom floor.
            Because doesn't he deserve it?
            Wouldn't you like to do that?
            To your husband?

CANDACE   I don't know.

NIA   What I'm trying to make clear to you, Candace, is
            that we don't have a choice.

We are compelled to do this.
It is inevitable.

CANDACE Yes.

NIA I just need to be sure that you fully and completely
understand that.
Because this is so important.
It is so –
Enormous.

CANDACE I know.

Pause.

What can I do?

Pause.

Tell me.
Please.
What can I do?

Silence.

NIA *is trying to compose herself.*

Nia.
Are you alright?

Pause.

NIA Sometimes…
It feels hopeless.

CANDACE Is *isn't* hopeless!
It isn't!

NIA Sometimes it feels as if I am achieving nothing.
That I am just…
Alone.
Futile.
Exiled.

Pause.

Sometimes that makes me feel very small.

CANDACE   You're not alone.
           You're not.

NIA   Perhaps.

CANDACE   Look.
           Come over tomorrow.
           We can talk properly then.
           I'm sorry about all that stupid stuff before.
           It's just bloody Miles and his…

NIA   I should let you go to sleep.

CANDACE   Oh I never go to bed this early.

NIA   It's after midnight.

CANDACE   You're still up.

NIA   Yes.
           That's true.

           Pause.

           What were you doing?
           Before I called.

CANDACE   I was drinking a glass of red wine.
           Just a cheapie one from M&S.
           And I was reading.

NIA   What were you reading?

CANDACE   One of my old favourites.
           The Portrait of a Lady.
           Lots of people find this one tricky.

NIA   I love Henry James…

CANDACE   Yes, I do too…

           Pause.

           What…
           What will happen?
           To the young man?

           Silence.

NIA   Goodnight.

CANDACE   I feel so –
           Hemmed in sometimes.
           Because I'm just an old woman.
           That's all I am.

NIA   No.
           You're not just an old woman.

CANDACE   I'm expected to act in a certain way.
           Speak in a certain way.
           I'm expected to say – of course!
           Of course you must run along and be with her and
           the two young girls you've been secretly
           supplying with sweets and potties and picture
           books for the last four years without my
           knowledge.
           Of course!
           Of course it is perfectly natural that you would fail
           to find me anything other than entirely repulsive
           now that I'm so faded and fat and completely
           invisible!
           Of course you would want to be with that young,
           lovely, *young* woman with her thick dark hair
           and her swan's neck and her elastic cunt!

NIA   I'm sorry.

CANDACE   Oh that felt good!

NIA   Yes.

CANDACE   You see sometimes I feel so completely stifled
           by –
           By politeness.

NIA   Yes.

CANDACE   I feel very angry quite a lot of the time.

NIA   I know.

CANDACE   I am quite often uncomfortably furious.

NIA   Yes.

CANDACE   When Evelyn died, do you know?
           I had fantasies about running people over in my car.
           Really crunching over their bones.

NIA   Do you still want to do that?

CANDACE   Oh no.
           Well sometimes.
           On bad days.

           Pause.

           I've been asking myself.
           Could I do something dreadful?
           If it mattered enough?

NIA   Well.
           It would depend how much it mattered.

CANDACE   Could I blow things up?
           Things and people?

           Pause.

           The things that have happened to you.
           If it had happened to me...

           Pause.

           I might be capable.

           Pause.

NIA   Goodnight, Candace.

CANDACE   Goodnight, Nia.
           Sweet dreams.

 # 14

YASMIN *and* A *are waiting for a bus.*

It's taking a long time.

A *has a shopping bag and is eating something from a paper bag.*

YASMIN *watches* A.

A *notices her gaze and smiles at her.*

A   Do you want one?

           Pause.

           YASMIN *shakes her head.*

           Go on.
           I've had enough anyway.
           I'm on a diet, supposedly.

           A *hands* YASMIN *the paper bag.*

           YASMIN *holds it but doesn't eat.*

           I'm starting to think this bus will never come.

YASMIN   Yes.

A   My daughter will be worrying.
           She's a worrier.

YASMIN   Yes.

           Pause.

A   Don't you want any of those?

           Pause.

           Well.
           You save them for later.

           Pause.

           Have you got somewhere to go?
           Love?
           Are you alright?

You'd tell me if you didn't have anywhere to go,
wouldn't you?

Pause.

YASMIN   Don't be nice to me.

A   What –

YASMIN   Cos if you start being nice I'll just...
Please.

YASMIN *hands back the paper bag.*

I need money.

A   Sorry?

YASMIN   Sorry it's just –
I have to ask you for money.

A   Um.

YASMIN   I need as much as you have.
Everything in your wallet.

A   Um.

YASMIN   And your phone.

A   Well wait a –
Wait a minute.

YASMIN   Sorry and I really don't want to have to do this
but –

She shows A that she has scissors.

I'm sorry.
But if you could give me your phone and, and all
your money that would be –
That would be very helpful.
I'm really sorry.

Pause.

I don't want to have to do anything to you but if
you don't give me what I ask for then I will, I will
have to...
I will have to hurt you.

Slowly A *hands over her/his phone, and a few notes.*

YASMIN *is still holding the scissors.*

Is that everything?

A   I'm, I'm sorry.
           This is everything –

YASMIN   That's all you've got?

A   I've been shopping so –
           I'm sorry.

YASMIN *looks at the money in her hand.*

YASMIN   I'm not really this kind of person.

A   OK.

YASMIN   You see I'm in this queue, for information.
           And they told me that if I had money they'd
           accelerate my request.

A   OK.

YASMIN   And you do anything, don't you?
           When it matters?

A   Yes.

           Pause.

YASMIN   I hope the bus comes soon.
           You've been waiting so long…
           I'm, I'm really sorry.

           They look at each other.

           YASMIN *exits.*

 # 15

ALI, *talking into a camera.*

He has rope around his ankles.

A, B and C, *all now in yellow dresses, watch him.*

ALI   I would like to –
Publicly –
Admit to my –
My deceit.

Pause.

The video of the girl in the yellow dress.
The girl who appeared to be shot and then bleed,
copiously.

Pause.

That video was in fact fabricated –
By me.
I am a...

Pause.

I am a film director.
I am a film director who also makes –
Porn films.

Pause.

My girlfriend...
Is an actress.
A...
A prostitute and, and a porn star.

Pause.

We concocted the film together.
In order to discredit and humiliate the
government.
Because we are traitors and –
And perverts.

Pause.

No one was shot that day.
No one is lying in a hospital bed with a tube in
their nose and a drip in their wrist.

Pause.

That is fiction.

Pause.

A fiction of our own making that we now –

Pause.

Bitterly regret.

Pause.

He removes his microphone from his shirt.

No.
I'm not doing this.

He starts to walk away from them.

A, B and C look at each other.

They shrug.

They pull on the ropes so he can't leave.

OK.
Very funny.

He tries again to leave but he can't.

So it's starting, is it?
Fine.
What's first?

C pops one of the yellow balloons.

OK.
OK I get it.

C pops another yellow balloon.

You can get on with…
With whatever you're going to get on with just as
soon as you tell me where she is –

C pops another balloon.

She had nothing to do with it.
I need you to understand that.
Can you just –
Nod, or say something, to tell me that you
understand that?

Nothing.

Is she next door?
Down the corridor?
Leyla?
LEYLA?

They pull on the ropes again.

He falls to his knees.

C *pins the microphone back onto his shirt.*

Smiles in a businesslike manner.

Points to the camera.

Smiles.

No.
I can't.

C *nods to* B.

B *hands* C *a mobile phone.*

C *shows* ALI *the mobile phone.*

He reacts violently.

He struggles to stand up.

They pull on the ropes.

He falls to the ground.

They make him look at the mobile phone.

He screw his eyes tightly shut.

They force his eyelids open.

He gasps.

Silence.

That –
That could be anyone.

Silence.

It's just…
It's just images…
How do I know you haven't –

He reacts to something on the phone.

He starts to weep.

C points to the camera.

Nods.

Taps the microphone on ALI*'s shirt.*

Wearily ALI *stands.*

They help him.

Pat his arms and smooth down his hair.

I would like.
To publicly admit to my deceit –

16

YASMIN *has a mobile phone.*

She dials a number.

Waits.

The line goes dead.

She breathes deeply then dials the number again.

A *enters with a large bag.*

She/he is still for a moment and then begins to unpack what is inside – pieces of cardboard and tape.

A *lays it out on the ground and looks at it.*

YASMIN *watches* A *as she waits.*

Finally somebody answers.

YASMIN   Hello?
I need to ask if there's been a registration of someone.
A, a woman.
Someone gave me your number, I paid him and –

Pause.

Wait please don't –

The line goes dead.

Hello?

Nothing.

YASMIN *slowly lowers the phone.*

C *and* B *enter.*

They watch A *unfolding the cardboard.*

B *and* C *look at each other.*

A   (*Handing them cardboard.*) Here.

Silence.

B   What's that for?

A   It helps.
If they, you know…

A *mimes a soldier with a truncheon.*

B   How do I – ?

A   I'll help you.

A *starts taping cardboard to* B*'s arms and legs.*

C *watches.*

YASMIN *dials a number again.*

C   My sister she –
She's got this bump on her head.

Pause.

We think she got hit with something, something
heavy, but she's not awake long enough to –
She just keeps sleeping.
I mean she wakes up for a bit and then, boom,
she's asleep again.
My mum is...

Pause.

She stood in front of the door, like a barricade,
and she –
She kind of begged me.
Not to go.

Pause.

She said, I don't know if it's worth it.
If I'm going to lose both of you.

YASMIN   (*Into phone.*) I think we just got cut off.
Yes, I told you, I paid.
I just need to know if she's been registered as –
Yes, I paid.

YASMIN *holds.*

C   I told her it is worth it.
It *is*.
It has to be.
Right?

A   If you don't want to come it's alright.

C   Because it's working, isn't it?
It's really working!

A   You should think of your mother.
We understand.
Don't we?

B *shrugs.*

C   I wasn't frightened yesterday.

YASMIN   Hello?
Yes her name's Marion.
She's fifty-five and she has a scar on her –
No please don't put me on hold again –

B   (*Holding out cardboard.*) Here.
           Come on.

YASMIN   (*Into phone.*) Yes.
           Yes I'm still here.

C   I just wish –
           I just wish she'd stop falling asleep.

YASMIN   N–
           No.
           That can't be right.

B   Are you coming or aren't you?

YASMIN   Can you check again?
           Please.

C   Yeah of course I am.

YASMIN   Check again.
           Check again.

           She reacts to something she hears.

           *She lets the phone fall out of her hands, squeezes
           her eyes tightly shut.*

           Stands there.

           C *starts wrapping yellow ribbon around her/his
           wrist.*

           YASMIN *looks at* A, B *and* C.

           *She looks at the ribbon they are winding around
           their wrists.*

           B *becomes aware of her gaze.*

B   Hello.

           Pause.

           Do you want one?

           YASMIN *nods.*

           Let me tie it on for you.
           Here.

YASMIN   I can manage.

           Pause.

           YASMIN *looks at the ribbon for a long time.*

B   It's easy to forget isn't it?

           Pause.

           I mean, that scrap of cloth...
           It could mean anything.

           Pause.

           But I feel like I know her.

YASMIN   You don't know her.

B   What?

YASMIN   You don't know her.

           Pause.

           YASMIN *digs in her pocket, finds something.*

           *She waits for a moments, then holds it up – it's a
           lighter.*

           She sets fire to the edge of the cloth.

B   Wait, what –
           What are you doing?

           YASMIN *watches it burn.*

           Stop that!

           YASMIN *holds the burning ribbon up high.*

A   What the – ?

C   Oh my God she isn't – ?

A   She is.
           She IS.

C   No – ?

B   How could you – ?
           What?

A   Who *are* you?

C   My God.

B   I don't understand.
         How could someone, how could anyone – ?

A   How dare you?

C   Stop it.
         STOP it.

A   People are dying.
         Do you understand?

C   Make her stop!

A   *She's* dying, do you get it?
         That girl is dying and this is the thanks you give
         her?

C   Wait.
         Give me your phone.

B   Huh?

C   People need to see this.

B   I don't know if that's –

C   Just give it to me.

         C snatches B's phone.

         Starts filming YASMIN.

A   Are you one of *them*?
         Are you?

C   OK.
         OK I'm filming.

B   Don't.

A   It's people like you that are holding back this
         fucking country, do you understand me?

B   Just let her go.

A   I don't understand you fucking people.
           Seriously.
           Why are you so afraid of progress?

B   It's not her fault.

C   Don't you WANT choices?

A   Why do we fucking bother?

C   Say something.
           Why don't you SAY something?

A   It might as well have been you.
           You with the gun.
           You that aimed it at her.
           You that pulled the trigger.
           You.

B   What are you doing?

A   Get hold of her, can you?

YASMIN   Get off me.

           YASMIN *lashes out.*

A   You disgusting, foul, pungent piece of SHIT.

C   Now hold her down.

A   That's it.

C   Got her?

A   We've got her.

           YASMIN *fights back with all her strength.*

YASMIN   It's a piece of cloth.
           Do you hear me?
           It's a piece of yellow cloth.

C   And now we SPIT on her.

           They spit on her.

           The sound of a huge explosion.

Everyone scatters, leaving YASMIN *alone on the ground.*

She touches her face, which is covered in blood.

She curls up and waits.

 # 17

CANDACE *with* A *and* B.

Outside a school.

CANDACE That's right, girls.
         You're coming with me today.

A   OK!

B   No we aren't.

CANDACE Didn't Daddy tell you?

B   No.

A   D'you have any crisps?

CANDACE Yes I've got LOTS of crisps actually.

B   But Daddy didn't tell us.

CANDACE Tsk, SILLY Daddy!
         Now, come along, that's it.

A   Silly Daddy!

CANDACE Your poor mummy's not feeling very well so she's
         gone to stay with a friend for a few days.

B   How many days?

CANDACE Oh just a few.

B   Has she got cancer?

CANDACE Of course not!
         She's got a little sniffle that's all.

A   *I* had a sniffle at the weekend.

CANDACE   Now I've got salt and vinegar AND I've got bacon!
           But chop-chop!

A   Salt and vinegar, saltandvinegarrrr,
             SALTANDVINEGAR!!!!

             B *puts her/his hands over her/his ears.*

B   Zoe, DON'T do that!

CANDACE   Now are you going to share with your sister?

A   NO!

B   We've only met you once.
             You kept crying.

CANDACE   What did you do at school today?
           Was it exciting?

B   No.
             It was school.

A   I did icebergs with Barnaby!

CANDACE   Icebergs!
           My word.

B   Why would school ever be exciting?

A   The *Titanic* hit an iceberg.

CANDACE   Yes it did.
           It certainly did.
           That's very clever.

B   You're walking too fast.

A   Lots of people drowned in the sea.
             Tiffany CRIED about it!

CANDACE   Oh dear, poor Tiffany!

B   You don't know who Tiffany is!

A   You're much older than our mummy.
             How old are you?

CANDACE   Ooh now that's a bit of a cheeky question!

A   Are you seventy?

CANDACE   No.

A   Our mummy is the prettiest mummy in my class!

CANDACE   Now, just a bit further, and we can hop into my car
and be off.

B   Are you a good driver?

CANDACE   I'm an excellent driver.

B   But you wear glasses.

A   *I* want glasses!
I want glasses and braces and I want to be a bit fat
too!

B   She watched a cartoon where the main character
was fat and had glasses and braces and now she's
obsessed with it.

CANDACE   How refreshing.

A   Do you have any children?

B   She doesn't.
I remember.

CANDACE   That's true.
I don't have any children of my own.

A   But all ladies have children!

CANDACE   There's a little boy called Suli who's going to
come and live with me soon.

B   Suli?

CANDACE   In fact I'm going to invite lots and lots of children
to come and live with me.

A   How many?

CANDACE   I don't know.
But lots.

A   I WANT TO COME!

CANDACE   Their country's in the middle of a sort of civil war
                at the moment, you see.

B   How far's your car?

CANDACE   Oh nearly there!

B   Mummy normally drives it right up to the school
                gates.

CANDACE   But the goodies might be starting to win, you see!

A   Are there baddies?

CANDACE   Yes.
                But a lot of them got blown up.

B   BLOWN UP??

CANDACE   Did I say that?

A   Did they get blown up into bits of tiny pieces?

CANDACE   I mean they got sent to sit on the naughty step.

B   We're not *babies*.
                The naughty step is SO STUPID.

A   Can I have the bacon crisps now?

CANDACE   Alright.
                Here we are!
                Now come along.

B   Your car's very dirty.
                You should have it professionally cleaned.

CANDACE   We can go through a car wash on the way if you
                like?
                They're always lots of fun!

B   Where are we actually going?

A   I want to sit in the front.

CANDACE   Uhhh.
                Yes you can sit in the front if you like.

B   Um, that is NOT allowed.

A   SHUDDUP!

CANDACE   Oh gosh.
           You'd probably better go in the back actually.

A   BUT YOU SAID I COULD GO IN THE FRONT.

CANDACE   Well that was a mistake.
           I shouldn't have said that.
           Of course children shouldn't go in the front.

B   Everyone knows that.

CANDACE   So can you please both just –
           Hop in, please.
           Quickly!

A   NO.

B   Oh dear.
           She's going to have a tantrum.

CANDACE   Now look.
           Little girls are NOT allowed to sit in the front,
           Zoe!
           Alright?

A   But you S-A-I-D.

CANDACE   It was just a joke!

B   I could have told you this was going to happen.

A   I want my –
           I want my M-U-U-UH-UH-M-Y-Y.

CANDACE   Zoe!
           Stop this nonsense and GET in the car.

A   NoooooOOOO.

B   She won't move now.
           Look, she's gone rigid.

A   I want my MUMMY.

B   I'll get in if that helps.
           Shall I?
           Would that help?

CANDACE *grabs* A *by the wrist and tries to manhandle her/him into the car.*

A   No!

B   You're hurting her!

CANDACE She's FINE.

A *screams.*

B *starts to cry.*

I've had just about enough of this.
Just get in the car.

A *and* B *sniff.*

GET in the car.

They refuse to move.

CANDACE *looks at them.*

They continue sniffing.

Something in her sags.

You're right.
I'm actually going to –
I'm actually going to take both of you back to the playground OK?

B   You are?

CANDACE Yes.
You see, I forgot.

B   What did you forget?

CANDACE I made a silly mistake.

B   A mistake – ?

CANDACE Your mummy's feeling much better and I, I, I got my days a bit muddled up so –

A   Mummy?

CANDACE So hold my hand and we'll just –

A   MUMMY!!!!

            CANDACE *freezes.*

            She can't move for a moment then –

            She runs.

 # 18

The GIRL *is in a hospital bed.*

YASMIN, *bruised and battered, sits in the chair beside her.*

The GIRL *stirs.*

She opens her eyes.

GIRL   Oh.
            Hello.

YASMIN   Hi.

GIRL   You're not a nurse.

YASMIN   No.
            Sorry.

GIRL   Do I know you?

YASMIN   I'm in the ward opposite I just –
            I shouldn't be here, I'll go –

GIRL   It's OK.
            Stay.

            Pause.

            The GIRL *licks her lips.*

            Got any lip stuff?

YASMIN   Um.
            There's some here.
            Want me to – ?

GIRL   Thanks.

            YASMIN *puts lip balm on her lips.*

            Pause.

            What's all this?

            She shakes her wrist.

YASMIN   There's medicine in there, I guess.

GIRL   Right.
            Would explain why I feel a bit –
            Wooo!

YASMIN   Yes.

GIRL   Bit cumbersome though.

YASMIN   Yeah.

GIRL   Oh well.

            Pause.

            What happened to you?

YASMIN   I had an accident.

GIRL   Looks painful.

YASMIN   Yeah it is a bit.

GIRL   We're in the wars.

YASMIN   Yes.

GIRL   We should be a bit more careful.

YASMIN   Yes.

GIRL   A boy hasn't been in here has he?

YASMIN   No…?

GIRL   No.
            Hey ho.

            Pause.

            You know, I just wandered out.

YASMIN   Sorry?

GIRL   The day I got…

YASMIN   Oh.

GIRL   I was curious.
I wanted to see what all the fuss was about.

Pause.

Some of my friends, they were all wrapped up in it.
They said, this is our chance!
They said, everyone needs to take to the streets
and fight for change!
They were so –
They were lit up by it.
I felt envious of all that –
Conviction.

Pause.

But I also felt like they were –
Acting?
Like I didn't quite believe their passion.
Does that make sense?

Pause.

Did lots of people die?

YASMIN *nods.*

Thought so.
You can hear in the corridors.
Screaming.

YASMIN   My mum did.

Beat.

GIRL   I'm sorry.

Pause.

Was she protesting?

Beat.

YASMIN   Yes.
           She was.

GIRL   That's so brave.

YASMIN   Yes.
           She was very brave.

GIRL   I just –
           I just went along to see.

           A crowd is starting to gather.

           What's that?

YASMIN   What?

GIRL   That noise.

YASMIN   Oh.

           Pause.

           People outside.

GIRL   What are they cheering for?

YASMIN   You actually.

GIRL   Oh.

           Pause.

           The GIRL *closes her eyes.*

           YASMIN *spots something under the bed.*

           She tugs at it.

           It's the yellow dress.

           It is cracked and sticky with dried blood.

           She studies it.

           She pulls the dress over her head.

           She goes to the window.

           She opens it.

She waves.

The sound of the crowd cheering.

The cheering becomes ecstatic.

The End.

A Nick Hern Book

Image of an Unknown Young Woman first published in Great Britain in 2015 as a paperback original by Nick Hern Books Limited, The Glasshouse, 49a Goldhawk Road, London W12 8QP, in association with the Gate Theatre, London

Image of an Unknown Young Woman copyright © 2015 Elinor Cook

Elinor Cook has asserted her right to be identified as the author of this work

Cover image: The Champion Agency

Designed and typeset by Nick Hern Books, London
Printed in Great Britain by 4Edge, Essex

A CIP catalogue record for this book is available from the British Library

ISBN 978 1 84842 488 3

Woodland
CARBON
www.woodlandcarbon.co.uk
NICK HERN BOOKS
Printed on Carbon Captured paper